Items should be returned on or before the date shown below. Items not already requested by other borrowers may be renewed in person, in writing or by telephone. To renew, please quote the number on the barcode label. To renew online a PIN is required. This can be requested at your local library.
Renew online @ **www.dublincitypubliclibraries.ie**
Fines charged for overdue items will include postage incurred in recovery.
Damage to or loss of items will be charged to the borrower.

Leabharlanna Poiblí Chathair Bhaile Átha Cliath
Dublin City Public Libraries

Comhairle Cathrach
Bhaile Átha Cliath
Dublin City Council

Due Date	Due Date	Due Date

THE
GENEROUS
GARDENER

THE
GENEROUS
GARDENER

Private
Paradises Shared

Caroline Donald

PIMPERNEL
PRESS LTD
www.pimpernelpress.com

CONTENTS

Pimpernel Press Limited
www.pimpernelpress.com

The Generous Gardener
Private Paradises Shared
© Pimpernel Press Limited 2018
Text © Caroline Donald 2018
Photographs © Caroline Donald except those
listed on page 208

A catalogue record for this book is available
from the British Library.

Designed by Becky Clarke
Typeset in Excelsior LT

ISBN 978-1-910258-97-2
Printed and bound in China
by C&C Offset Printing Company Limited

9 8 7 6 5 4 3 2 1

Frontispiece: Luciano Giubbilei's
border at Great Dixter.
Page 8: Penelope Hobhouse's
Somerset garden.

Introduction 6

NATASHA SPENDER 10
Provence

CHARLES SHOUP 14
Peloponnese

HENRY CECIL 18
Newmarket

WILLIAM WATERFIELD 22
Menton

JANET WHEATCROFT
& SHERPA DAWA 26
Dumfries & Galloway

DAVID & BELLA GORDON 30
Pays de la Loire

JOHN HARRIS 36
Monmouthshire

PETER HARGREAVES 39
Somerset

GERRY & HEATHER ROBINSON 44
Donegal

LORD CHOLMONDELEY 49
Norfolk

CHRISTINE FACER 54
Gloucestershire

JULIAN & ISABEL
BANNERMAN 58
Gloucestershire

WILL ALSOP 62
Norfolk

SHIRLEY SHERWOOD 66
Oxfordshire

ANDY HULME 72
London

BOB FLOWERDEW 76
Norfolk

JOHN & JENNY MAKEPEACE 80
Dorset

JILLY COOPER I 84
Gloucestershire

NEIL ARMSTRONG 88
Cornwall

WILL FISHER 92
London

ANA TZAREV 96
Cap Ferrat

JUDITH PILLSBURY 100
Provence

LORD CARRINGTON 106
Buckinghamshire

SAM MCKNIGHT 110
London

WILLIAM CHRISTIE 115
Pays de la Loire

JIM CARTER
& IMELDA STAUNTON 119
London

CAROL BRUCE 124
Kent

LADY MOUNTBATTEN 128
Kent

STUART ROSE 132
Suffolk

HARRISON BIRTWISTLE 136
Wiltshire

JILLY COOPER II 141
Gloucestershire

LUCIANO GIUBBILEI
& FERGUS GARRETT 145
East Sussex

NEISHA CROSLAND 150
London

CORINNE BAILEY RAE 154
Leeds

CATHERINE FITZGERALD
& DOMINIC WEST 158
London

ROY LANCASTER 163
Hampshire

KELLY BROOK 167
Kent

Introduction to Part 2 173

PENELOPE HOBHOUSE 174
Somerset

TESSA TRAEGER
& PATRICK KINMONTH 180
Devon

LOUISE DOWDING 185
Somerset

MICHAEL LE POER TRENCH 190
Somerset

DAN PEARSON & HUW MORGAN 194
Somerset

CHRISTOPHER GIBBS 198
Tangier

Gardens open to the public 203
Index 204
Acknowledgments 208

INTRODUCTION

Each to their own, and all that – but you can count me out of the current penchant for extensive tattoos. To me, it would be like wearing the same piece of clothing every day, for the rest of my life. And I'd get mighty bored of it.

And that is why I like gardening. With gardening – and here it differs not only from having your forearm covered with mystic symbols, but also from painting a picture or even decorating a room – you are creating something in which your own efforts are only one element of what you see and experience: the show doesn't stop, just because you do. Even in the most ordered of spaces plants grow, plants die; they spread and you can move them around, or even get rid of them. The garden is always slightly beyond your control, doing its own thing in its own time. The gardener sows a seed, plants a bulb or a tree and then just has to wait – days, weeks, months, even years. Every season the place will look slightly different, depending on what the weather throws at it and what is happening around it and how you tend to it (or not). That's what makes it exciting, with something new to experience every time you pass through.

'I think gardening makes people happy, don't you?' said Penelope Hobhouse the other day, as we sat on her terrace in the summer sunshine, cocooned by a jungle of plants and pots. Well, yes, when it comes down to it, I would agree, whether it is haute horticulture and design as practised by Penelope, or just planting up a window box outside your flat with some herbs for the kitchen. That's the essence of it. It can also make people unhappy – all that responsibility and hard work, guilt and frustration when things don't go to plan, and sometimes huge expense. It may not feel like it on a chilly March day with mulch to spread, but, for those of us in a position to choose, gardening is a luxury and a privilege. Most of the gardens in this book are in the British Isles, where the climate continues to be douce, if a little unpredictable. There is (usually) plenty of water, enough sunshine, and highs and lows of temperatures that are bearable. We also a have a huge range of readily available plants that grow well here, without too much effort. If we are unable to tend our patch, or choose not to and let the brambles and the bindweed take over, it may be distressing to witness, but nobody is going to die. Precious ornamental plants may wither to nothing if left untended, but there are always exciting replacements to be discovered in our garden centres and network of wonderful nurseries. Vegetables may be at the mercy of slugs, deer, pigeons and rabbits but the greengrocers and supermarkets are well stocked, and you won't starve. You can even make it a political statement if you want – go organic, indulge in a spot of guerrilla gardening, or question the established order by means of landforms and art – but you are not going to be clapped in prison for expressing these beliefs.

And, if tending to a garden is really going to make you miserable, well then, don't bother: buy a flat, or, if you must have an outside space, plant a few low-maintenance shrubs and cover the place in plastic grass. Or just surrender to nature and convince yourself you are creating a wildlife sanctuary: the local fauna would probably be rather more grateful for this than a well-tended patch anyway.

It is my belief that gardening is the indigenous – and democratic – art of the British Isles; the nation's 'folk art', in which everyone of whatever class or age can participate and express themselves freely.

The French have their cooking, the Italians their pride in their appearance, the Americans their Halloween costumes, and much of the world can converse happily about football, but gardening – along with the weather – is the firm glue that sticks the Brits together, a neutral territory of interest that includes rather more women than discussing the Premier League.

In what other country would an annual horticultural event like the RHS Chelsea Flower Show occupy so many hours on national prime-time television and newspaper column inches? Plus, a few plants cost considerably less than a season ticket at Stamford Bridge and you will probably get more exercise cutting the lawn than sitting in front of the telly shouting at the ref. And then there are the thousands of gardens open to the public, either as businesses or for charity: even the lowliest allotment can join great acres as one of the 3,700 or so gardens open for the National Gardens Scheme.

Gardening certainly makes me happy, whether it is pottering around in my own, a quarter of an acre of densely planted, barely organized chaos surrounding my cottage in Somerset, or admiring other people's efforts. It comes to us all – eventually. At *The Sunday Times* newspaper, where I have been gardening editor since the turn of the millennium, young colleagues who have hitherto been more interested in swigging back the beers and flying to Fez for the weekend get to the stage in life where they own some outdoor space. Instead of group selfies in far-flung places, they now bring me photos of their patios with the pride of new parents showing off their progeny, and it is delightful. Whether their busy lizzies in a beer barrel are to my taste is irrelevant: they have Got the Bug and it will stay with them for the rest of their lives.

Although many of the people featured in this book are well known, in the end, they are just people, like anyone else, who love their gardens. Going back over the interviews I have done for *The Sunday Times* over the years (and adding a few new ones), has been a heartening experience, one for which it has been worth abandoning my own borders to the weeds for a few months. I can remember each encounter: how welcomed I was made to feel – which is not a privilege accorded to those in many fields of journalism – how ungrudging the owners were with their time and knowledge, feeding me and often sending me away with a pot or two of plants (I did check with an editor if I should declare a couple of courgettes and some French beans when the new anti-bribery rules came in); how patient they were with my endless follow-up queries. Most of all, I remember their pride in sharing what

they had created, commissioned or inherited and perhaps a little quiet chuffdom that it was considered interesting enough to be featured in a national newspaper – never, ever boastful; Mr Toads would not be countenanced between these covers.

So, this book is as much about my own pleasure in revisiting these moments, and the later contact with the owners to find out what has happened in their gardens since my visit. I have called it *The Generous Gardener* in their honour, for that is what they have been. Some of the gardens may be open to the public on a regular or occasional basis for the National Garden Scheme and otherwise (there is an index of these at the back of the book) but they are all the result of the seeds of a private passion sown. And the fact that 'The Generous Gardener' is also a beautiful rose, named by David Austin Roses to mark the seventy-fifth anniversary of the NGS, that most generous of English festivals, makes it all the more appropriate. I have the rose in a prime position in my own garden. Due to mixed labels, it wasn't actually the one I thought I was picking up from the garden centre but it has more than earned its place with its fragrant pale pink flowers, which have the good grace to keep going for months.

There are many paths through a garden, and which ones their owners take is what interests me – rather more, I confess, than plantsmanly detail as to what is in it, though of course that is an important element. Whether it is Bob Flowerdew growing an abundance of fruit and vegetables for his family in Norfolk, with his unique approach to aesthetic appeal; Dan Pearson, one of the world's leading designers, carving out his own quiet place on a hillside near Bath; or Judith Pillsbury, an American art dealer who bought La Louve, a living work of art in Provence, their plots have brought them great joy.

There are those whose gardens are primarily for themselves – for example, Carol Bruce, who has created her own microcosm of order in Kent; or they may be for the public and posterity – Tremenheere, Neil Armstrong's exciting new landscape with sculptures in Cornwall, or the Bannermans' redesign of the walled garden at Houghton Hall in Norfolk for Lord Cholmondeley, in memory of his grandmother Sybil Sassoon. And, showing there is always something to learn, however many accolades you have won, Luciano Giubbilei, Chelsea gold-medal-winner, has discovered the power of flowers at a mature point in his career and is experimenting with a border in a corner at Great Dixter, learning from Fergus Garrett, master of floriferousness, and others there.

Perhaps the most cheering are those who would not immediately spring to mind as garden enthusiasts – among them Kelly Brook, the tabloids' sweetheart; singer Corinne Bailey Rae; and Peter Hargreaves, founder of the Hargreaves Lansdown investment platform. They may have busy careers elsewhere, but they still make time for their gardens and care deeply about them.

In this present world of disquiet, unrest and unease, the quiet joys of sowing, digging, pruning, and even just sitting still for a few moments in a green space away from everything, seem ever more important. Gardening does indeed make people happy. And for that, if nothing else, it matters.

Somerset, August 2017

Natasha Spender

Provence

Natasha Spender's Provençal neighbours along a quiet country road near Maussane-les-Alpilles scratch their heads when asked directions to Mas St Jérôme, her French home for nearly forty years. They have no idea where it is – have never heard of it or her – until a man chopping wood down a dirt track exclaims: 'Ah, the English writer!' and gives directions back up the track.

It is easy to see how Lady Spender, now eighty-four, and her late husband, Sir Stephen, the poet, who died in 1995, could have managed to live in the area so inconspicuously for so long. The garden surrounding Mas St Jérôme is a mass of trees and shrubs that blends almost imperceptibly into the olive groves and craggy limestone countryside of the Alpilles region around it.

Natasha Spender's garden was made famous by the publication in May 1999 of her book *An English Garden in Provence*, a beautifully written record of how she and Stephen had built up Mas St Jérôme from a ruined farm-house surrounded by impenetrable brambles, and how she had created her garden single-handedly from scratch. It was also a loving account of the life she and Stephen had led there since buying it in 1964 for £500 as a place in the sun. The names of illustrious friends, including Iris Murdoch and John Bayley (annual visitors for twenty-five years – 'I adored them,' she says), Francis Bacon, David Hockney, Leonard Woolf and Vita Sackville-West pepper the text, along with useful information about how to create a garden in a terrain with a very limey soil, long hot dry summers, biting mistral winds and occasional hard frosts.

Natasha Spender, at the window of Mas St Jérôme.

In July 1999, just two months after the book came out, disaster struck. Stephen's biographer John

Sutherland and his wife, Guilland, were staying at Mas St Jérôme. 'I sleep very well during the first three hours of the night,' says Spender, whose room is at the front of the house. 'Guilland went to the bathroom at 12.30 a.m. and saw flames from the back window in the direction of St-Rémy [-de-Provence]. She roused me and I called neighbours who live down there. They said, "For God's sake, get out; we can smell it, we can hear it crackling and we are leaving at once."'

The Mas St Jérôme party did the same. 'I owe my life to Guilland, because if I had been here alone I wouldn't have woken up,' says Spender. She took only a few possessions, including a Greek icon of St Jerome himself, given to her by her husband: 'I just wonder whether if I had left him in the house, he would have taken care of it,' she muses.

The fire, which was fanned by the mistral winds that whip down the funnel of the Rhône valley, left both house and garden almost devastated. 'When we drove back in the morning, we didn't think it looked so bad,' says Spender. 'Only one or two trees in the olive orchard were affected. Then we turned the corner and I could see sky through Stephen's window, so I knew the roof had gone.' She had lost two thousand books – and much else – in the fire, but was philosophical about its effects. 'The Sutherlands were much more upset than I was,' she says. 'They somehow thought they could have done more and I had to absolutely insist to them that they had saved my life.'

Spender ascribes her fortitude to having lived through the Blitz in wartime London. 'People expected me to move on,' she says, almost surprised at the thought that it might be a bit much for an octogenarian to rebuild a razed house and garden. 'But what else would I do? This is the only house I own. My life has been here, as it has been in St John's Wood [her London base]. We have been here for forty years and I think where you live is very important. I notice that widows very often feel a double pang when they are uprooted.'

So, she remained firmly rooted and, four years on, the house is rebuilt, she has restored the garden almost back to its old glory and is adding another chapter for the paperback edition of her book. 'I consulted the Royal Horticultural Society the day after the fire,' she says, 'and they said, "Do nothing. Just leave everything and see what survives."' Sure enough, something of a phoenix has risen, especially in the *maquis* garden, the shrubby area in front of the house, which is designed to lead the eye gently from garden to landscape and where many of the plants have sprung back to life.

On closer inspection, the garden still bears scars – the burnt lower branches of the cypresses in the lilac walk have been removed; a beloved *Acer griseum* foundered after the fire, and disease has finally claimed a ceanothus. The surrounding white limestone crags, sketched over and over again by Stephen from his bedroom window, are denuded of the pines that used to pepper them. But, ever positive, Spender sees these losses as an opportunity to open up new vistas and install new occupants.

Far from putting her feet up and enjoying her restored garden, Spender plans to take advantage of the demise of a pine-tree windbreak and is extending the terracing up the hill, with the help of her gardening friend Janette Coleman. '*Arbutus andrachnoides* doesn't mind the wind and has a wonderful cinnamon-coloured trunk. The ones we have put in are already shooting up,' she says, 'and I want to have parasol pines, so we will have to make sure there is enough good earth there. They don't burn as badly as the Aleppo pines (*Pinus halepensis*).' (Indeed, it was the Aleppo cones that spread the fire damage in the garden, as, when they were alight, they flew through the air like fireworks.)

Last winter there was an exceptionally hard frost, which has added to the damage in the garden – the lovely big shady mulberry on the terrace was so badly affected by the combined effects of fire and frosts that it will probably have to go, and Spender lost a precious fremontodendron. 'I have brought another one from London,' she says, not to be defeated. 'And I am just havering about where to put it, whether it is going to be too exposed.'

She drives down to Provence from England, carting many of the plants in the back of the car. In the garden around a raised pond, the roses have been brought over from Peter Beales's nursery in Norfolk. 'It used to be nothing but 'Super Star' and 'Peace' in the nurseries here, although there are one or two places where you can buy shrub roses now.'

Despite having little experience when she first arrived at St Jérôme in the 1960s, she was determined to have a garden there, and did her homework thoroughly – Stephen may have loved the garden, but it was always her project. 'I just sat around looking at the site,' she says. 'Harold Nicolson was still alive then, and he told me that they had waited four years before they decided on the axis of the garden at Sissinghurst. I went around to see the plants that did well in the wild – I went quite far afield, to the limestone uplands in the Gard and Languedoc and to the Luberon. I thought of the cultivars of the species that did well in the wild.'

Spender decided to eschew the formality of grander houses in the area. The pomegranate hedge in the rose garden, for instance, is left unclipped. 'I don't really like those tailored hedges,' she confesses. 'For one thing, the whole idea here is to merge the garden into the countryside. And the area is so beautiful that anything formal would look rather ridiculous.' So, for example, lavenders planted at the garden's edge mirror the grey foliage of the olives beyond.

Although when she is not at Mas St Jérôme the house is looked after by guests and house-sitters, she can't really expect them to spend their days tending the garden; so Spender's approach of making sure she uses plants that are thoroughly suited to the surroundings also works well in maintenance terms. 'If you plant the natural things, they are going to be happy.' Not that this stops her considering new additions to the garden. 'I am too old to have love affairs,' she laughs, 'so I have love affairs with plants. Sometimes I can think of nothing else.'

26 October 2003

Natasha Spender died on 21 October 2010, aged ninety-one, having been too frail to garden at the Mas St Jérôme for the last three or four years of her life. The property has been sold to a young French couple, who are planning to restore the garden.

The restored garden, showing little sign of the devastating fire damage.

CHARLES SHOUP

Peloponnese

O n first impression, it's as if the millennia have rolled away in Charles Shoup's garden at Cavogallo. Built along and above a third of a mile of the rocky, unspoilt shoreline of the Bay of Messinia in the Peloponnese, the eight acres of shady terraced garden hark back to the days of Plato and Socrates.

Not for Shoup the expensive, incongruously lush, watered lawns and orderly planting favoured by modern-day wealthy Greeks. The gardens surrounding his impressive nine-bedroom neoclassical villa – a reference more to a revivalist style fashionable in the early nineteenth century than to the original of ancient times – are composed of courtyards, paths, axes and formal vistas, with not a blade of grass in sight. This is not a climate in which lawns thrive without considerable assistance and expense.

Shoup has planted five thousand trees, including olives, parasol pines, cypress, citrus and palms, plus decorative specimens such as jacarandas, which provide much-needed shade in a climate that sees little rain from April to September and where temperatures can reach 40C. Most are evergreen, many are clipped into balls and columns, and they provide sturdy structure both during winter and in the dog days of summer.

As the property sits on top of limestone walls, built to stop the erosion of the shore, the height above the coastline gives it some protection against the battering of the sea. Along the front of the garden, salt-tolerant species – for example, *Metrosideros excelsa* and *M. robusta*, both of which have red bottlebrush-like flowers – provide a windbreak and a barrier against the waves. 'Nobody local seems to know the wind-resistant qualities of metrosideros,' says Shoup. 'And it is absolutely unaffected by seawater. It starts flowering in December and goes on until the beginning of August.'

Raised in New York state, where the family money came from department stores, Shoup, who is in his late seventies, was in the same class at Yale as George Bush Sr. After wartime service in the US navy, he left America as soon as he could, living in Paris, Venice, Tangier and the south of France, earning his keep as an artist.

'I was a painter; I wasn't a very good painter but I was very successful,' he says. He tells of life on the Riviera, of painting John Paul Getty and amusing lunches with Noël Coward – 'the most charming person I've met in my life. He was more fun than a barrel of monkeys' – Winston and Clementine Churchill, William Somerset Maugham and other 'sacred monsters', as he calls them, borrowing from Jean Cocteau. However, 'To be a portrait painter, you had to be social. I got very sick of all that, so I came to Greece to get away.'

Despite its beauty, the Peloponnese – the large hunk of land at the southernmost point of mainland Greece – is a far from fashionable part of the country, which is how Shoup likes it. Patrick Leigh Fermor, the writer, may live across the bay, but the smart set tends to head off for Spetses and other islands.

Shoup's first property in the Peloponnese was within the walls of the castle at Koroni, visible across the bay from Cavogallo. He bought the castle for $150 (then equivalent to £35) in 1959 and lived there for twenty-five years. He still owns it, and one of his staff lives there. He bought the land for Cavogallo in 1962 for $7,000 (then £2,500). 'It's very difficult to buy land on the sea nowadays,' says Shoup – he says that it now fetches about £27,000 a stremma (the local unit of land, roughly equivalent to a quarter of an acre).

Charles Shoup, on the grand steps leading down to the first courtyard at Cavogallo.

The pebble beach below the garden is reachable only by sea or from the cove's few properties. It has provided material for a mosaic terrace seat and pebbled steps that lead to a viewing point over the bay. The seat has been created recently by one of his three gardeners and is a painstaking labour of love – although the task must have made a welcome change from watering the hundreds of pots that adorn the courtyards and steps.

The mosaic work is the latest of many projects that have kept Shoup busy on the property over the years, as well as working as an architect – he drives up to Athens every week. When he bought the land, it was terraces overrun with brambles – 'they used to burn it every year.' He started planting the garden in 1971 and built the house in stages between 1971 and 1985.

The house unashamedly shows two fingers to modernism, the prevalent taste at the time, and in fact both it and the garden have benefited from Shoup's anti-fashion stance. As his contemporaries destroyed the grand neoclassical nineteenth-century villas of nearby Kalamata to make way for contemporary buildings, in would come Shoup to snaffle up classical statues, old pantiles, balustrading and even walls, as in the shady 'Turkish garden' at the side of the house, bought in an Athens flea market.

'Everything is rescued from demolition; I bought them for nothing at all,' says Shoup, who is obviously keen on saving things. At one time he had twelve dogs, rescued as strays – he now has four. His architect's eye is evident both in the house, which is built in a U-shape around a central courtyard, and in the garden. A path leads from the courtyard up through terraces lined with olive trees underplanted with white irises, clipped columns of teucrium and balls of pittosporum, cypresses neatly trimmed as if into columns at an ancient acropolis. At the path's end is a formal arch and a pool and, beyond, a statue of Demeter, the goddess of agricultural fertility. Shoup goes to stand beside her: she is tiny, but his clever *trompe l'œil* scaling of the steps in front of the statue makes her look bigger than she is, and the garden appears to extend further than it does.

Other tricks are employed, too: the house's portico, for instance, hides a flat roof and ugly solar panelling that heats the water. At the top of the long flight of steps leading up the hill from the first courtyard is a triumphal arch, based on Hadrian's arch in Athens. Anyone with the energy to stagger up there will find a rewarding view of the bay. If they look under the arch, they will see it holds a water tank for the garden, itself a triumph in that the property has its own stream, which supplies that most precious of commodities in a Mediterranean climate. 'I wouldn't have bought it otherwise,' says Shoup.

Indeed, water is plentiful in the garden: two stone troughs in the first courtyard are alive with bullfrogs that croak loudly all day and night, while in the central

Above left The statue of Demeter is in fact tiny, but the *trompe l'œil* scaling of the steps in front makes her look much bigger, so giving the impression that the garden is longer than it actually is.
Above right Pots of all sizes punctuate the dense planting in the central courtyard.

one, beyond the large carob tree that dominates the space, a simple fountain both cools the air and draws the eye to the archway beyond, which frames views of the sea.

The time has come for Shoup to sell Cavogallo and find somewhere smaller. It is unlikely to go overnight, so he and his dogs can enjoy this self-made arcadia of shady terraces and the ever-present sound of the bullfrogs for a little longer.

16 July 2006

Cavogallo was sold not long afterwards to a Russian, who pulled it down. Shoup has recently designed a neo-Palladian house in New Koroni and has moved in, aged ninety-one.

HENRY CECIL

Newmarket

'Smell this,' says Henry Cecil, as he shoves a sumptuously purple rose under my nose. 'It's nice, isn't it?' Underneath the whiff of tobacco from his fingers – the eminent racehorse trainer smokes Marlboro Lights constantly as we stroll around his garden near Newmarket – there's a heady, peppery evocation of a summer evening.

Cecil, one of the greatest trainers British racing has ever seen, and whose speech is like rapid bursts from a machine gun, professes not to know much about gardening, let alone roses, but it's clear he loves the planting at his Suffolk home, Warren Place. He entrusts it to Gordon Harvey, who has been with him for more than twenty-five years. 'You'd be amazed at how much he does,' says Cecil. 'Hours mean nothing to him. At four in the morning, when it is pitch-dark outside, you can hear him doing something with the lavender border, or he's spraying. He hardly ever takes a day off.'

Warren Place was built by the Maharaja of Baroda in the 1920s, and is a Tudorbethan creation of plaster and old ships' timbers. 'It's a very homely house,' says its owner warmly. Around it are thirty acres, of which about ten are devoted to the garden – he has never worked it out exactly.

Not long after the champion trainer bought the place in 1977, he and his first wife, Julie, planted hundreds of French, English and Chinese roses. 'We designed it together twenty-five years ago: I used to know every rose in the place, but I don't now. I don't think the soil in this part of the world is the best place for them, as we are on chalk. But certain ones do very well.'

Cecil has always loved gardens. As a boy, he spent most of his holidays at Crathes Castle, near Banchory in Kincardineshire. Now in the hands of the National Trust for Scotland, the baronial pile was then owned by his mother's family. 'It has one of the best gardens in Scotland. My grandmother and grandfather were amazing gardeners – they used to bring back all these plants from abroad. When I was a child, there were about ten gardeners there.'

In his large, productive kitchen garden, he shows me some exotic 'mummy' peas. 'A relation of my stepfather, Sir Cecil Boyd-Rochfort, introduced Howard Carter to Lord Carnarvon, and they all went over to the Valley of the Kings. Out of one of the mummies fell four or five peas. Boyd-Rochfort put them in his pocket and took them back to Ireland. After 2,500 years, they germinated. I think I'm now the only one with these peas: they are very sweet, twice the normal size and very light green.'

Even this area contains rose borders, filled mainly with old-fashioned varieties, and Cecil's equine charges (he has about sixty in training) have their

Henry Cecil, dressed down, in front of Warren Place.

own rose hedge. 'We decided to put a rugosa rose right round the whole fillies' yard. Instead of giving them a peppermint or a sweet, you've got all the hips here. The fillies love the hips.'

He rides out every morning for about four hours, which must account to some extent for his deep tan and slim figure. As we visit his indoor riding school, we discuss shoes – he has about two hundred pairs – and shopping. 'I'm a compulsive shopper,' he admits. 'I could shop all day in London from nine o'clock to seven at night. Clothes, or pictures, or presents. I think I've probably got female hormones.'

Cecil has another predilection commonly considered feminine: flower-arranging. He cuts blooms for the house himself, and many of the roses he points out as favourites, such as the pale pink 'Queen Elizabeth', are long-stemmed. There is no shortage of vases, as his dining room sideboard is groaning with cut-glass racing trophies.

Modern roses come into their own indoors. 'They are so easy to stick in a vase when people come to stay,' he says. He shows me the green and pink 'Pierre de Ronsard', which comes from an abbey in France. 'They are quite expensive; I bought quite a few last year and gave them away as Christmas presents. Pretty, aren't they?'

Not all varieties pass muster: 'One I can't stand is 'Joseph's Coat', all orange and red.' He could also live without the famous yellow-pink Hybrid Tea 'Peace', named on the day Berlin fell in 1945, though he'd hate to offend those who do like it: 'It's a matter of opinion; it's got a history.'

The garden is not just about roses, though. 'I love geraniums,' says Cecil, inviting me to admire some specimens. We inspect his glasshouses, hung with melons, muscat grapes, figs and white peaches. Dotted around the expanses of lawn are specimen trees including catalpa, arbutus and magnolia. The magnolias are a particular favourite and by the front door is a little purple *Magnolia* 'Jane', planted in honour of his girlfriend, Jane McKeown. 'Pretty, isn't it?' he says, seeking approval one last time.

6 August 2006

The double borders of roses and lavender provide ample material for Cecil's flower arrangements.

Henry Cecil died in 2013, aged seventy, having married Jane McKeown in 2008. In 2012 his friends Louis and Mark Massarella presented him with the creamy Floribunda rose 'Sir Henry Cecil' and a certificate of naming as Christmas present. The message read: 'Our request was for a rose which encompasses hardiness, great character and resilience: qualities which only you and the very best possess.' It is available from Handley Nursery and can be seen in front of the main entrance to the July Course at Newmarket racecourse, planted in the great trainer's memory. 'Henry particularly enjoyed the three-day summer showpiece at this atmospheric course,' Jane writes. 'At this meeting some of the roses are made into buttonholes, which I present to the winning connections of a Listed race that is run annually in his memory.'

The rose is also planted in the family graveyard on the Crathes estate, where Cecil is buried. 'I'm so pleased, as I think Henry got his love of roses and gardens from his grandmother, who helped to create the wonderful gardens at Crathes Castle,' writes Jane.

Warren Place is now owned by His Highness Sheikh Mohammed bin Rashid Al Maktoum, Vice President and Prime Minister of the United Arab Emirates and Ruler of Dubai, who is founder of the Godolphin stables.

WILLIAM WATERFIELD

Menton

A bearded man in a scruffy sweatshirt is raking leaves as I walk up the hedge-lined drive of Le Clos du Peyronnet, in the smart Garavan area of Menton, on the Côte d'Azur, a stone's throw from the French/Italian border. Nobody answers the doorbell, so I approach the gardener to ask where Monsieur Waterfield, the owner, would be. No need for French, however, for it is he – he had been so absorbed in his task that he hadn't noticed the visitor approaching.

In fact, there is no gardener other than William Waterfield, apart from the occasional student sent for a week's practical work. He maintains the densely planted one and a half acres of terraced hillside himself. It is one of the finest private gardens on the Riviera, a secret jungle of rare plants, winding paths and hidden corners with an elegiac air of glory days gone by.

Waterfield, who is now sixty-three, moved to Menton thirty years ago. He is the third generation of Waterfields to live at Le Clos du Peyronnet, a yellow-washed Italianate villa with a wisteria-covered pergola along its front facade, built in 1897 and bought by his grandparents in 1912. It sits on the site of a much older house in a walled area (hence 'Le Clos') and there are olive trees in the grounds that are seven hundred years old.

Waterfield's brother Giles wrote *The Long Afternoon* (2000), a novel based loosely on their grandparents' life in Menton. For much of the last century, the Riviera was the hangout of wealthy, cultured expats – Earl Haig, commander in chief of the British Expeditionary Force on the Western Front, owned the house in front; Winston Churchill and Noël Coward took villas to enjoy the mild winters; Katherine Mansfield, Lesley Blanch and Graham Sutherland all lived here. Waterfield remembers meeting Clive Bell, a leading member of the Bloomsbury Group. 'He came here when I was a little boy. He was a portly figure, waistcoated in the way people were in those days.'

Many of these wealthy expats were keen gardeners, and they exercised a friendly rivalry with each other. Those days have gone, however, and the Corniche, once one of the smartest roads in the world, is now clogged with camper vans and coaches. When I ask if there any of the old set left, Waterfield replies 'Me. There is a huge pressure to sell your house so they can build a block of flats instead.' He has resisted, though part of the house was divided into flats by his father and uncle, and the garden remains.

In his grandparents' day, the hillside garden was nothing to write home about. Being close to the border with Mussolini's Italy, the house had been badly bomb-damaged in the war when Waterfield's Uncle Humphrey took it over. 'The

William Waterfield, pictured on my second visit to Le Clos du Peyronnet, in 2017.

garden was in a very poor state,' says Waterfield. Humphrey gave it its bones, including the five-pool water cascade that leads the eye down the hill and out to the Mediterranean beyond. He was a great friend of Lawrence Johnston, owner of nearby Serre de la Madone and of Hidcote in Gloucestershire (though one suspects watchfully competitive eyes, on both sides, as they created their patches of paradise).

Around the garden are pieces and plants from other gardens, a reminder of times and friendships past, including a stone bench, with the words Viva Il Duce carved into it, probably by a bored Italian soldier using his bayonet when stationed at Serre de la Madone. Uncle Humphrey later bought the bench from Nancy Lindsay, to whom Johnston had left the garden, and it is now installed at Le Clos du Peyronnet in a prime position for sea views.

Waterfield read botany at Oxford but paid little attention to the horticultural aspects of the course. What green fingers he acquired came through experience rather than books. 'My parents were keen gardeners – and Uncle Humphrey,' he says, adding with typical modesty, 'Everyone thinks I'm an expert, but I've never had any formal training. I've got quite efficient about looking after things and

The world in a garden.
Above Exotics such as aloes, *Dasylirion wheeleri*, cacti and *Dracaena draco* thrive in the douce climate of Menton.
Opposite A glimpse of the Mediterranean, through the dense planting around the series of ponds created by Waterfield's Uncle Humphrey.

watching them die expertly and with resignation.' In fact, he is known as one of the best plantsmen in the Mediterranean, with a particular expertise in South African plants (including a large collection of bulbs in pots), brought back from his travels. He follows his uncle's maxim of 'good plants, well shown'. 'My ideal thing to have is something immensely rare that looks stunning and is totally adapted – some wonderful Chilean bulb nobody else has.'

The climate at Menton is the best on the Riviera for gardens, though Waterfield misses typically English plants, such as delphiniums, which don't thrive. 'Even if it did grow, it would be a travesty.' And, although nurseries plug it, frangipani fails too: 'It's just too cold – though there is nobody more optimistic than a nurseryman.'

This report was written in 2006.

I revisited William Waterfield on a damp day in March 2017. His wife, Judith Pillsbury, former owner of La Louve (see page 100), was away and we walked round the garden in the rain. It was as abundant as ever. There are now two gardeners and, despite Judith's inclination to cut everything back and impose some order, there is still a luscious, jungle-like feel to the place. That's not to say there is disorder: Waterfield has kept a meticulous record of everything he has planted over the forty years he has been living there.

JANET WHEATCROFT
& SHERPA DAWA

Dumfries & Galloway

If Janet Wheatcroft and her husband, Andrew, had moved to a house other than Craigieburn, near Moffat in Dumfries and Galloway, in 1983, several lives would have been very different. The climate in their six-acre garden, nestled under Hunterheck Hill and by the waters of the Craigie burn, is warm and moist, perfect for growing plants from the Himalayas. So Wheatcroft set about creating a garden based on these plants, and in 1995 she trekked to Makalu in Nepal to collect some from their natural habitat.

A Sherpa, Daten Ji – known as Dawa – was assigned to look after her. It was the monsoon season and, as they crossed a river in full spate that had,

Dawa and Janet Wheatcroft, in front of a photograph of the Dalai Lama on the bothy door.

says Wheatcroft, 'boulders the size of cars' hurtling down it, the rock she was standing on began to slip. 'This is it,' she thought. 'I am going to die in this godforsaken place.' Dawa was also in trouble, but managed to keep his cool and get them both to the other side. 'He just wouldn't let go of me; he had been told to look after me and that was that.' Wheatcroft's brush with death affected her profoundly, not least in her gratitude to Dawa for saving her life. She promised to invite him to Scotland so that he could improve his English.

Once back home, she found the garden at Craigieburn was becoming overwhelming. 'It was just chaotic,' she says. 'I couldn't find anyone to do it. It was a real low period in my life.' She kept her promise, however, and Dawa came to visit Craigieburn in 1997. He had never previously been out of Nepal. 'He came over for six months on a visa, and we became fantastic friends,' says Wheatcroft. 'I was trying to get the garden round and he would help. It didn't take me long to realize that he has an instinctive knowledge of where a plant wants to be. Because he has been used to planting on a mountainside, he knows how to deal with big, rocky gardens with no soil. "I make soil" is his mantra.'

Dawa's visits became regular, in between escorting ascents of Everest and other expeditions. And in 2002 his wife, Ang Diki, and three of his children (one is at boarding school in Kathmandu but visits in the holidays) joined the Wheatcrofts at Craigieburn. Dawa is now studying horticulture at nearby Barony College and uses Craigieburn as his practical work placement. Ang Diki helps in the house, and the children are at the local school.

Dawa and Wheatcroft have created a lovely, peaceful garden, with formal areas in front of the house. These include two wide summer herbaceous borders, a rose garden and spaces enclosed by yew hedges. Further out the garden becomes more wild and loose, with bog and woodland areas.

Dawa, whose English is still on the idiosyncratic side, is very proud of the fact that he uses only Nepalese tools (his favourite being his hoe), apart from secateurs, a hand saw and a 'little pushing mower'. 'This whole garden I have done on myself,' he says, a statement that Wheatcroft generously lets pass, though she has had her fair share of getting down on her knees with a trowel.

Dawa and his family may be a long way from home, but Nepalese culture is much in evidence here. As you enter the garden, you pass under fluttering prayer flags hanging over a stupa, and a former gardener's bothy is now a little Sherpa house, complete with Buddhist shrine and a photograph of the Dalai Lama.

The plants, too, are reminders of home: the blue Himalayan poppies that flower in early summer are the most popular with visitors. The giant lily *Cardiocrinum giganteum* is also a prominent feature when it flowers in July. 'Janet showed me it and I said, "This is everywhere in Nepal,"' says Dawa. 'The book says you need to wait seven years for flowering, and when they flower they are 7 feet tall. Then they die back and you need to wait three years for the second flower. Absolute rubbish. Every single year we get flowers – they were 16 feet tall last year.' To prove his point, he has kept the plant's dried stalk.

Dawa has planted twenty cardiocrinum in his new Nepalese garden, complete with prayer wheel, in a steep gully leading down to the burn. Here are reminders of his home that British gardeners now take for granted, such as arisaemas, bamboo, bergenia, meconopsis and roscoeas. He cleared the whole area of brambles and clinker using only his Nepalese hoe.

When I ask who is in charge of the garden, they point at each other and laugh. There is the occasional falling out, as both are strong characters. 'That is one thing I always say when I get peeved: "It's my bloody garden!"' says Wheatcroft. 'He then goes into a black mood and the whole family go, "Oh God, have you and Dawa fallen out again?" But we get on pretty well. It's the sort of friendship where you can have flaming rows and it doesn't really matter.'

13 August 2006

Andrew died in October 2016, and Dawa dressed the wicker coffin with an abundance of late flowers from the garden. The Sherpas went to the funeral in full Sherpa dress, and Dawa wrote a special song – he is a famous singer in Nepal. 'It was such a moving thing, not a dry eye in the house,' writes Wheatcroft.

The pair are still working together at Craigieburn; Wheatcroft has made over the garden business and nursery to Dawa, and he bought the former cafe from her to make into his family home. They also continue to have the occasional skirmish over the garden.'The rest of the family dive for cover until it blows over, and then wonderful things come out of it – creative dissonance,' she reports. 'Life is never dull and we are so proud of our garden.'

It is not only the plants that are reminders of the garden's Himalayan connections. Prayer flags adorn the bothy (opposite) and the stupa (above) near the entrance to the garden.

DAVID & BELLA GORDON

Pays de la Loire

The architectural beauty of spent seed heads, such as those of allium, acanthus and echinops, standing alongside later-flowering perennials and grasses, has long been appreciated by fans of what could loosely be described as the new European school of planting. It's a style that relies on perennials planted in an environment in which they will thrive, and so they will be easier to look after.

But to the French this *laissez-faire* approach is still novel. According to David Gordon, of Plantagenet Plantes in Anjou, the local attitude remains more: 'We are going to plant annuals, and if the cannas need to be watered four times a day, then that's what we will do.' It is his and his wife Bella's mission to show the French, with the utmost *politesse*, that there is another way. To this end, the Gordons have made a beautiful, relaxed garden at their farmhouse in Argentay, a hamlet near Saumur. Their nursery, which is also based there, takes its name from the counts of Anjou, who became the Plantagenet kings of medieval England.

An undulating fence, made from the wooden posts that used to stand at the end of rows of vines in the fields around the farm, marks the barrier between the public space for nursery visitors and the family's private territory. Limestone walls surround a gravel courtyard and create a warm, sheltered microclimate. The soil is chalky and free-draining.

The climate here could be compared to that of south-east Britain at its best – albeit with shorter winters – and there is a similarity between the Gordons' creation and those one might find in England. They are aware, however, that it is not a template for all their French customers. 'As you go further south, the colours get much brighter, which has a certain logic to it, as the sun gets stronger,' says David.

Those inspired by the gardens they might have seen in England can sometimes make mistakes. 'People have visited Hidcote or Sissinghurst and think they are fantastic. Then they go back to somewhere south of Limoges and use the same colours in their planting scheme. It's too soft, and the plants all get burnt in about five minutes.'

It is the Gordons' aim to guide their French customers to the right plants for the right place. Their Argentay garden is a good example: growing through the wooden posts are the striking purple 'Wunder von Stäfa' aster and self-sown *Verbena bonariensis*. Golden hazes of *Stipa tenuissima* partner dusky pink sedums; the tall fronds of *Stipa gigantea* planted beside rusty echinaceas and double rosy pink Japanese anemones catch the low late-summer light; the fluffy

David and Bella Gordon, in front of the farmhouse they rescued from near-dereliction.

plumes of *Pennisetum orientale* 'Karley Rose' meld with a cloud of delicate gaura. It's like the rich colours of a well-worn Persian carpet.

The couple moved to France in 1997. They met when they were both working at the BBC in London and found they shared a love of things horticultural. While others might have arranged trips to the cinema or a restaurant, their idea of a hot date would be to visit a garden. But there was obviously more to the relationship than discussing obscure varieties of salvia and sedum, as they eventually married.

After their first child, Beth, was born (now ten, she has since been joined by Luke, seven), they again decided to follow their hearts. 'We always said that we would run our own nursery one day, and really it was our daughter who was the catalyst,' says Bella. 'Suddenly we didn't want to live in London any more with a little baby. We thought: let's do this nursery thing now.'

A house with enough land for a nursery proved prohibitively expensive and well nigh impossible to find in the south-east of England, but the Gordons had an alternative in mind. 'We always had a vague idea that it would be nice to live and work in France,' says David. 'We felt that there was a market there for selling unusual perennials and to try to give advice and design.'

They rented in the area, then found a dilapidated farmhouse with outbuildings and ten acres of land, which they bought for about £45,000 in 1998. 'This is the growing area of France,' says David. 'They call Anjou the Jardin de France, and between Angers and Tours is where all the big nurseries are. It is a nice area. It is very mild and you don't really have extremes of climate.'

Although surrounded by fields of vines – for this is also wine-making country – the Gordons are not completely in the sticks. 'It's very accessible,' says David. 'You can get to Paris in an hour and ten minutes on the TGV, for example. It's not too far from Britain for going back or for friends coming out. In terms of just the practicalities of running a nursery, we have got all the suppliers and everything like that round here.'

The house may have been in a barely habitable state but, having sorted out the kitchen and a bedroom, their priority was to get the horticultural business up and running. Relying on passing and local trade in a sparsely populated rural area, where your *jardin* is your vegetable patch, was never going to bring the euros flooding in, so the couple set up a mail-order business for the plants they grow at the nursery.

'We didn't want to be a small, specialist, marginal operation – we needed to make the nursery big enough to support a family,' says David. 'We don't want to have to work all the time and never have enough money – it wasn't just pursuing a hobby. We thought: we have to make enough money out of this to buy the children shoes and occasionally go on holiday.'

As is obvious from their own garden, the Gordons have an eye for design. They have incorporated this into their business. 'You couldn't just sell the plants, because the French had never seen them before, though they have more now,' says Bella. 'That's why we did the garden and how we got into design work.'

Low evening light catches the sedums, grasses and seed heads

They readily admit they have the advantage of being big fish in a small pond, though one suspects they would survive pretty well anywhere. In France, the garden design industry is still small. 'You get a chance to do really interesting things here, because there is nobody else to do them,' says Bella, modestly.

'It's still relatively rare in France to work as a garden designer with a private client,' she says. 'In Britain, the number is huge. There are a lot of French words for cooking, but there are a lot more English words about gardening and garden designers. It's just a sign of the cultures.' Even the French word for a designer, *paysagiste*, is telling: 'It could be anyone, from someone who rakes leaves to a person who designs the garden.'

About 75 per cent of the nursery's turnover of plants is wholesale, supplying other designers and landscapers and working on municipal projects. 'There's a very big market there,' says David. With two years of drought, water is becoming an increasingly important factor, and local authorities cannot be seen to douse their plants with the precious resource while they impose restrictions on residents. 'If it's dry, then you plant what would be happy in those conditions; you don't try to plant gunneras, then water them eight times a day,' says David. 'It's very basic stuff.'

The drought has kept them busy, even teaching other professionals at the internationally famous park and garden conservatoire at Chaumont-sur-Loire. 'We teach them to use perennials as glorified annuals but to leave them in place,' says David. 'Or we try to persuade them to do more natural styles of planting. In that case, we ask, "What are the conditions you've got?" and we choose the plants accordingly.'

There are times off-season when the Gordons might question what they have done, but moments of homesickness soon pass. When Bella celebrated her fortieth birthday with thirty guests, dining on trestle tables in the courtyard, there were old English friends but plenty of new French ones, while hordes of children played around them. Local wines kept the revellers well watered. Like the plants in their garden, the Gordons seem to have found an environment in which they thrive.

17 September 2006

A decade on, the Gordons have stopped selling online in order to concentrate on their design work, for which they also supply the plants. They are kept busy, largely by the increasing numbers of wealthy Parisians buying in the area and wanting a garden that is low maintenance and eco-friendly. They also continue to design and supply public projects, such as the entrance to the new Lascaux caves museum and municipal planting at the regenerated town of Pantin, to the north-east of Paris.

In their own garden, the courtyard is now largely planted with evergreen shrubs, in order to provide year-round interest for visitors, while the drifts of perennials have been moved behind the house. They have taken dual British/French nationality: 'We'll certainly stay here until the end of our careers,' says Bella.

Verbena bonariensis, asters, sedums and grasses bring low-maintenance colour and structure to the farmyard.

JOHN HARRIS

Monmouthshire

Dewstow House, near Caldicot, in south Monmouthshire, is a pleasant, if not particularly grand, five-bedroom country farmhouse, probably eighteenth-century, with a smart Victorian facade and stone balustrade slapped on the front.

Its real value, however, is in the goldmine of horticultural history that surrounds it. A seven-acre garden was laid out in the late nineteenth century by James Pulham & Sons, one of the leading landscaping firms of the day, but for decades it lay buried under concrete, spoil and bramble thickets, before being unearthed by its current owners.

John Harris bought the house in 2000 and lives there with his wife, Lisa, and their three young children. He was no stranger to the property, having lived next door all his life. His grandfather, William, had become manager of the Dewstow estate farm in the 1940s; in the 1950s, when the estate was carved up, he bought 250 acres and farmed it as a family concern.

As for the gardens, 'We knew something was there, but not how far it extended,' says Harris. 'It had all been buried for fifty-odd years.' Elderly locals recalled visiting as children on open days; they told of domed glasshouses filled with rare plants and tropical birds. Even though there were few photographs and no records, there were still clues to past glories, such as the fancy pillars in the Dutch barn (a remnant of the enormous glasshouses that once lined the back wall) and the hint of a grotto at one end of the sloping farmyard.

'We started digging in various areas to tidy it up,' says Harris. 'There were blocked-off passageways in one of the grottoes. Once you open up tunnels and other areas, other tunnels start appearing and on you go. We didn't know what we would find.'

What they eventually unearthed was a rock garden with a warren of underground chambers beneath, all varying in style and some top-lit through a glass roof. The 'rooms' include a fernery, with pillars of fake volcanic rock, and two palm courts – one with formal balustrades, the other with a pool. A tunnel leads to what was once the tropical glasshouse.

In front of the house is another tunnel, which opens on to a wide, shallow ravine, its clay lining suggesting it was once a bog garden. There is also an Italianate formal area and, towards the outer edge of the garden, a series of ponds forms part of a reticulated water system that feeds other features.

'The visible ponds were in a bad state,' says Harris. 'One of them was used for drainage off the road, so it was full of diesel, gravel and cracks.' Other ponds, buried under 12 feet of soil, were also dug out. 'They were in better condition, though they all leaked terribly, so we have had to reseal the lot. The Italian garden was not completely buried, but it had had cattle and horses running over it for fifty years, so the walls had all crumbled and the ornamental stuff was either smashed or had gone.'

The gardens had been commissioned by Henry Oakley, a director of the Great Western Railway, shortly after he bought the 600-acre Dewstow estate in 1893. A bachelor recluse, Oakley spent his money on the garden. His pockets must have been deep, as James Pulham & Sons was the fashionable firm of the day: Sandringham, Waddesdon Manor and the RHS Garden at Wisley are all examples of their work, as are the gardens of Buckingham Palace.

The firm's speciality was creating naturalistic landscapes of rocky out-crops and ravines. If they couldn't find the right boulders – granite, tufa or stalactites – skilled craftsmen created them from Pulhamite, a mix of concrete render and a rubble or brick base. The rock shapes were so cleverly fashioned that they looked like the real thing.

John Harris, on a restored wall in the former farmyard.

When Oakley died in 1940, the house passed to his solicitor, Stanley Naish, who employed John Harris's grandfather, William, to manage the estate. Britain was at war, and the needs of a productive farm took priority over horticultural fancies: Oakley's pride and joy was left to go wild. Then the estate was broken up, and the fate of the subterranean gardens was sealed, literally, when thousands of tons of spoil from the building of the nearby M4 were dumped on top, to a depth of 15 feet. An orchard was planted in one section; the rest was concreted over.

The Harrises farmed their 250 acres until 1987, when the family firm diversified into golf. 'We started in a small way, with a 9-hole course and a driving range,' says Harris. 'Now two 18-hole courses have gobbled up all the farmland. The second course opened in 1995, and that was the end of our farming.'

John Harris's purchase of Dewstow House reunited the estate's original holdings for the first time in fifty years.

As they have no idea of the original planting scheme, Harris's gardeners have improvised, using ferns and palms in any of the subterranean gardens with enough light to sustain them, creating a lush jungle atmosphere. Above ground, an Edwardian pastiche has been rejected; instead, there are modern herbaceous

A subterranean grotto in what, were it not for Harris, could have been forever a lost world.

borders, full of toning colour, drama and variety. The Italianate formal area is adorned with tulips and box hedging.

Harris estimates that uncovering and restoring the lost gardens of Dewstow has cost about £250,000. But he is proud not to have sought a penny in grants towards restoration, even though their Grade I listing means the gardens are eligible. He has had them restored primarily for his family to enjoy; however, they are open to the public five days a week, to cover running costs and to let others see this extraordinary legacy of Edwardian opulence.

He is clearly horrified by the idea of Dewstow becoming the Welsh equivalent of Cornwall's Lost Gardens of Heligan, swarming with coach parties and facing the concordant demands of increased facilities, staff, insurance and bureaucracy – not least because he lives in the middle of the gardens.

It has been a horticultural odyssey, although Harris admits his knowledge of gardening remains minimal. 'I'm not a gardener, and I don't know much about gardens, but I really like this one. It was curiosity that got it going. Excitement carried it on, but, pretty soon, it got to the stage where the extent of it was much more than we had imagined.'

29 April 2007

The Harris family has sold the golf course and John and his wife are concentrating on running the gardens as a business. With thirty thousand visitors a year, their dreams of a quiet life have had to adjust. Who knows what else lies beneath the soil? But they have stopped looking – for now.

PETER HARGREAVES

Somerset

Does a garden allow you to detect something of its owner's character? Even if I didn't know who owned the grounds I am strolling through, it would be difficult to look at the strong shapes of the lush foliage, the perfectly manicured lawns and well-tended shrubs, and not conclude that it was owned by a man – and, one might suspect, a captain of finance?

In this patch of Somerset countryside, blowsy flowering borders are for wimps, weeds are banned and green is good. The man behind this horticultural tight ship is Peter Hargreaves, co-founder, with Stephen Lansdown, of the Bristol-based fund manager Hargreaves Lansdown. It has been a profitable venture: earlier this year, he is estimated to have made £80 million by selling off part of his holding, and his remaining 32 per cent stake has been valued at more than £300 million.

Stinking rich he may be, but Hargreaves is also very much the bluff Lancastrian, with a friendly, down-to-earth manner and a broad accent reminiscent of another keen gardener, Alan Titchmarsh. (In fact, he grew up about thirty miles north of Titchmarsh territory, which is over the border in Ilkley, Yorkshire.)

'We haven't tidied up especially for you. You could have come on a surprise trip and you wouldn't see a weed on the site,' he says as we set off at a cracking pace around the garden. The pressure is on: Rose, his wife, is cooking an early dinner for the couple and their two teenage children, Robert and Louisa, as she is off to a salsa class.

'I'm quite pleased with what we have here,' he says, as we carry out our whistle-stop tour. I suspect that, understatement regardless, he's really very chuffed. What Hargreaves has is impressive, even though the garden is not, he admits, as large as those owned by some of his horticultural buddies.

'There's a joke among all the people who are into gardening big time,' he says. 'You ask, "How big is your garden?" They reply, "Manageable". That means about seventeen acres.' It is a game he has learnt to play. 'When they ask me, I say I've got a very small garden.'

The anecdote reveals something of the circles in which Hargreaves moves. His four-acre cultivated garden, surrounding an elegant seven-bedroom nineteenth-century house just south of Bristol, is scarcely pocket-sized, and there are another eighteen acres of pasture beyond.

The planting is all about foliage, sweeping verdant expanses and architectural structure. 'I'm not really a flower man,' he says. 'Unless you're Beth Chatto, I don't think you do terribly well with herbaceous. It's a lot easier with shrubs. Perennials can look so dull if they're not well done.'

Colour concession: Peter Hargreaves, in front of the perennial border, planted since my first visit.

Indeed, to paraphrase Henry Ford, the plants Hargreaves generally favours come in any colour, so long as it's green.

'It depends what you like,' he says, admitting that the horticultural scheme he has adopted is not for everyone (and that apparently extends to his wife, Rose, who 'goes mad' that there aren't more flowers). 'This is a garden 365 days a year,' he says. 'Take away the few areas of flowers and the colours are still fantastic to me; there are ten shades of green – at least.'

The main view from the house is of a wide lawn, edged with shrubs, with an 80-foot tulip tree to one side. It's the perfect spot on which to erect a marquee – in fact, there would be room for a couple of them – but scarcely private for a spot of down-time. So Hargreaves has plans for a sunny corner near the walled garden. 'We are going to make it into a sundial garden. We'll find its geographic centre and shrub it all the way round. My wife will be able to sit in there during the day without being disturbed by the gardeners.'

There are three of these, headed by Terry Seavers, who lives in the lodge at the end of the drive. Hargreaves may not do the double-digging, but he is very much involved in the decision-making. 'I do the logistics, and have a lot of input, because if you don't do that, you don't get a garden.'

Although Hargreaves's muscular approach to planting can seem a little short of *joie de vivre* in places, his argument about the power of foliage really comes

Shades of green in the parterre in front of the house.

into its own in the lower section of the garden. Reached through an archway, a series of Victorian terraces lines steep slopes down to a stream. Here, the garden closes in: the planting becomes more dense, the tones and shapes provide more contrast and texture, and the subtle differences are more accentuated. Spikes sit alongside wide, shining jungle leaves, russets contrast with silvers and golds, and dense hedges give way to airy climbers.

Rhododendrons, azaleas and conifers are interspersed with more exotic tropical plants, including Chusan palms, cordylines, gingers and even bananas, despite the fact that this is a frost pocket. They are planted in a series of different areas and, as we walk through, the effect is a little like a world tour. The use of bamboo, acers, statues and a slate path gives a vaguely Far Eastern feel, and the area did start out as an Oriental garden, although this mood, its creator admits, has been somewhat lost in recent years.

A large gazebo is reached by a small boardwalk across the stream. 'It was so big, we thought it would dominate the place,' he says. 'We used to call it the bandstand.' Now, however, it is covered in fast-growing Virginia creeper, framed behind by bamboo and tall paulownias. Hargreaves likes to lurk unseen in there on the occasional days when he opens the garden to the public – usually to aid local charities – so he can hear what people think. 'Nobody has ever been rude about it,' he reports.

A wood-framed glasshouse lines the wall leading to the working area of the garden, behind the house. This is full of potted plants and, later in the year, will protect some of the more delicate outdoor specimens. It is a lovely piece of Victoriana, but, sadly, its days are numbered. Although the front windows were fixed a few years ago, it is considered beyond repair and has been marked for demolition.

Through a gate in the wall are a yard and a new greenhouse, for which Hargreaves has big plans. 'We are going to grow aubergines, tomatoes and peppers in here. I like red peppers, I think they're fun,' he says, as if contemplating a new toy. The place is gardened organically, and there is a large and productive walled kitchen garden.

The nearest thing to flash – in terms of colour, rather than money – is in a sunny spot to the back of the house, near the compost heap. Here, perhaps in deference to his wife's views, is a bed specifically designed to grow cut flowers for the house: it is a riot of dahlias, gladioli, chrysanthemums, crocosmia and nerines – all perfect for the late-season vase. Rose has notched up another small victory. She is being allotted an area by the drive in which to create a rockery, where she will grow miniature tulips, irises and narcissi, as compensation for the scarcity of blooms elsewhere.

Hargreaves doesn't delegate everything. Rather surprisingly, given his views on flowers, he organizes the hanging baskets of red busy lizzies that line the veranda. He also grew the plants for the box parterre by the house from cuttings he took himself – although he confesses that he didn't grow and shape the topiarized spirals.

He is planning another hands-on project, although he freely admits that he might not have the patience for it. He has bought a holly which has been trained in the Japanese style – bare stems and leaves finely clipped into cloud-like shapes – and is planning to copy the technique. This is certainly ambitious. Large examples of the art form sell for thousands of pounds and – more important, as far as Hargreaves is concerned – take years to achieve. 'That is why it is not me, perhaps,' he explains.

Still, it is not as though he lacks the ability to build something out of nothing. According to its founder, Hargreaves Lansdown has become the biggest unit-trust broker in Britain 'by a wide margin' since it was set up twenty-six years ago. Closer to home, the garden was in a pretty sorry state when he and Rose moved to the property in 1996.

Other than the mature trees, which were already in place, everything has been planted since. 'We used to joke that we had the national weed collection here,' he recalls. 'It was unbelievable. Right up to the fence was a complete wilderness.' That might account for his dislike of weeds.

But again, there is something of an inconsistency. As we head back to the house, I spy a small patch of self-sown seedlings messing up the path underneath a 150-year-old box tree. Are they destined for the spray gun? Er, no. It seems this ostensibly hard-nosed horticulturalist isn't above bending the rules a little: 'We leave them there for a little bit of fun.' Not weeds as much as a spot of intentional disorder.

16 September 2017

Serious pruning, wall training and raking in an area that has reclaimed its oriental flavour.

Ten years on from the original article, I contacted Peter Hargreaves to see if he minded if I used the article in this book. He felt that it had been a bit unfair: the garden is far more colourful than I had written (though, in my defence, it has developed considerably since my visit). So back I went for a look, and I am pleased to report that yes, there is plenty of colour, most strikingly in a new border full of grasses and perennials. He has also created several other new areas, including a tropical garden, which zings with reds and pinks, and a gravel garden. There's also what he calls a Triassic garden, which has a steel model of a stegosaurus, lying among tree ferns, a stumpery, rhus and cycads (so still pretty green).

Hargreaves has now largely retired. The garden has to contend with golf for his time, but he is still planning new areas.

GERRY & HEATHER ROBINSON

Donegal

The station clock may keep perfect time, but the train departures from Oakfield Park station, in Donegal, depend on human whim rather than a timetable. The engine that draws out of the spanking new shed is as likely to be steam as diesel, while the carriages, painted in the colours of the original Donegal railway, are somewhat cosy in scale.

And the destination? The nearby town of Raphoe, perhaps? Londonderry? Dublin? Nope, it ends up back at Oakfield Park. For this is a miniature railway, built to take visitors on a three-mile journey through forty-five of the property's hundred acres of lakeside, landscaping and newly planted Irish woodland trees, including oak, ash, alder, willow and hawthorn.

The railway is the big boy's toy of the entrepreneur Gerry Robinson, who was born in Donegal. His parents emigrated to London when he was young,

and he rose through the ranks from the cost office in a toy firm to become one of Britain's best-known businessmen. His wife, Heather, is the one who sorted out all the details of the railway, such as the original Raphoe train tickets and the old timetables and posters that decorate the waiting room. 'The boys have tramped on my territory,' she jokes, as Robinson insists he drive the engine to take us round the estate.

'Why did we do it?' ponders Robinson, amused at the suggestion that building your own railway might be considered a bit bonkers.

Left All aboard the Raphoe express: Gerry Robinson in the driving seat.
Right A view across the lake towards the house, once the deanery to the local cathedral.

'It started because the piece of land that we bought is oddly shaped, and we thought a train would be a good way to get people round. Then it became a steam engine, which is fun.' Heather isn't convinced. 'It's almost embarrassing,' she says.

An open day in August at the estate attracted 3,500 visitors, hundreds of whom queued for a ride. The railway, along with a gothic-style folly – built beside one of two lakes, on a two-thirds scale to make it look further away – may border on the eccentric, but Robinson is too keen a businessman to throw his money away on a rich man's indulgence. The estate is open sixty days a year. 'There is an open garden scheme in Ireland that allows you to offset some of the costs against income tax,' he says. 'It is a good way to get large private gardens open to the public. That drove us a bit.'

Robinson, who holds a British passport and was knighted in 2004, has a long history in business. In 1987, he led the UK's then-largest management buyout, the £163 million purchase of what became the Compass Group. He joined Granada in 1991 and became its chairman in 1996. He has also been chairman of BSkyB, Arts Council England, ITN and Allied Domecq.

More recently, he has become known to an audience beyond the business community with his BBC television series. In *I'll Show Them Who's Boss*, in 2004, and *Can Gerry Robinson Fix the NHS?*, earlier this year, he displayed his considerable charm, as well as tough management techniques. At present, he

is filming a follow-up to the latter series at Rotherham General Hospital. He is also chairman of Moto, the motorway services group. 'I like the balance of the two,' he says of his dual media and business careers. 'It's like gardening – if you don't have to do it, it's really fun.'

For many years, the couple lived in west London and had a holiday cottage in Donegal. While Robinson still travels to London regularly, Oakfield Park is their main home. They live there with their teenage children, April and Tim. (Robinson has two other children from his first marriage; his daughter, Samantha, lives on the estate with her daughter.)

Last year, the beautifully restored seven-bedroom eighteenth-century house won Viking Irish Garden of the year, and earlier this year it was a runner-up in the *Country Life* Genius of the Place award. Yet when Robinson bought the property in 1996 from Billy Patterson, a member of a local singing troupe, the Pattersons, it was far from prize-winning. The two acres of walled former kitchen garden were 'just a field – there were cattle in here,' says Robinson. It is now divided into sophisticated, formal 'rooms' in different styles.

Neither Robinson nor his wife claims to be a gardener, yet they had a strong idea of what they wanted. The house, almost French in style, with newly restored lime plastering and a deep slate roof, was built in 1739. It served as the deanery for the cathedral in Raphoe for more than a century before it passed into private ownership. (Robinson, a Catholic, spent several years at a seminary in his teens.) The couple enlisted the help of Tony Wright, an architect from Northern Ireland who had been involved with the National Trust, to work on the house and garden. 'We were looking for someone who would be sympathetic to the age of the place and its history,' Robinson explains. 'He was a real find. He had a good sense of what should be.' Wright's wife, Elizabeth, helped with the original planting scheme.

The house and formal areas are situated at the top of a gentle slope, looking out at the front on to a wide lawn surrounded by woodland, with Croaghan Hill beyond. At the bottom is a small ornamental lake that Robinson had dredged and restored. To the side of the house is an immaculately clipped box parterre, designed to be viewed from the windows above.

A narrow path cuts through the parterre and across a large expanse of wildflower meadow, leading to a small pavilion. Usually, when wealthy men say they 'built' something (as in 'Henry VIII built Hampton Court'), they mean that someone else did the dirty work. Not so Robinson: he may not have green fingers, but he is handy with a hammer and nails. He built the single-roomed structure himself, using elm from the estate that had fallen victim to Dutch elm disease. 'My dad was a carpenter, and it probably represents something for me,' he says.

Nor is the pavilion a one-off: there are several other constructions of Robinson's around the estate, including a boathouse on the lake below. 'I lost

The gothic folly is built on a two-thirds scale, to make the lake look larger.

plenty of bits of tools in the lake making that,' he says. He also likes to work on the trees on his property, pruning and maintaining the planting. The parkland does not, however, live up to its name. 'In the 1950s, a local wood distributor bought it, stripped it of its oaks and sold it again,' Robinson says. 'I met him and said, "You bastard." He replied, "No, that's just what you did back then."' To replace the ravages of the woodland raider, the Robinsons have been planting new oaks, with seven permanent gardeners and casual summer labour to do the work.

'We are hoping to have as many species of oak as will survive,' Robinson says. 'We are up to 130 or 140, and there are something like 300 species.' Some of these, Heather points out, 'don't even look like oaks.' All in all, the couple have planted about 60,000 trees. 'They were originally put in as whips,' Robinson says. 'They are a mixture of hollies, limes, a lot of beech, oak, chestnuts and stuff like that.'

So, is there a conflict between the Robinsons about how the estate should look? 'Gerry loves his lines and the big lawns,' Heather says. 'I like the wild woods and the bluebell woods.' 'Heather would have the place less formal,' adds Robinson, though he admits he can see the charms of her approach. 'What is great about a place like this is that it had been farmed and there were cattle all over the place, so everything got eaten. But we have had this amazing resurgence of bluebells and all kinds of things under the trees. The idea that all this stuff is already in the soil and grows back is very pleasing for Heather.'

The couple have taken a fine house with beautiful established parkland and made their own mark in a way that does it proud. 'There is something about a place with a bit of history,' Robinson says, as we pass an avenue of mature beeches. 'You go through the woods very happy with what has already been done. It is hard to believe the stuff you have planted will end up with it. The great thing about redeveloping old houses is that it absolutely does remind you how transient it all is.' And, as Heather adds, 'You are just a moment in the lifetime of all this.'

18 November 2007

Much has been added at Oakfield Park since my visit, including a new railway-based tea room and restaurant, largely built with fallen timber from the estate. There are now several sculptures dotted around the garden and Robinson has added to the rolling stock on the railway with another closed carriage and a 'Royal' carriage. A Christmas Santa Express event attracted more than sixteen thousand visitors in its first year. Robinson writes: 'However, I think the main secret that is now out is that, despite her protestations, Heather has shown her true colours as being the real rail enthusiast among us.'

LORD CHOLMONDELEY
Norfolk

David Cholmondeley, 7th Marquess of Cholmondeley, Earl of Rocksavage, Earl of Cholmondeley, Viscount Malpas, Baron Cholmondeley of Nantwich and Joint Hereditary Lord Great Chamberlain (and that is just his British titles), is intrigued as to why the new garden dedicated to his grandmother at Houghton Hall, his 4,000-acre estate near King's Lynn, in Norfolk, has been named Historic Houses Association and Christie's Garden of the Year, 2007.

'I can't think why we have been voted in,' Cholmondeley (pronounced Chumley) says of the award. 'There are so many gardens with so much going on in this country.' Such modesty belies what Peter Sinclair, executive secretary of the HHA, calls 'an amazing achievement': the creation, over the past seventeen years, of an impressive garden in the five-acre walled former kitchen garden, which lies beyond the stables to the south of the house.

Cholmondeley inherited the estate, which draws twenty thousand visitors a year, on the death of his grandmother in 1989. A few months later, his father, Hugh, the 6th Marquess, died, and he inherited Cholmondeley Castle, in Cheshire, and the surrounding 7,500-acre estate, where his mother, Lavinia, still lives. 'It was a busy time,' he says, with understatement. As well as looking after both houses, he also makes films: the latest, *Shadows in the Sun*, shot in Norfolk and starring James Wilby, is awaiting release. *The Sunday Times* Rich List for this year estimates his fortune at £60 million, although much of it is tied up in art.

Cholmondeley's grandmother was born Sybil Sassoon in 1894, the daughter of Sir Edward Sassoon, of Baghdadi Jewish Indian lineage, and Aline de Rothschild. A formidable woman, she was a superintendent of the Women's Royal Naval Service during the Second World War. 'She was a clever woman, a great linguist, and she loved literature, music and painting,' Cholmondeley says. When Houghton opened to the public in 1976, 'She got really keen on it, sitting selling guidebooks on the house. She loved that – she loved talking to people. That's what kept her young at heart.'

Although interested in gardening, Sybil and her husband had other concerns. 'They had plans for a water garden,' Cholmondeley says. 'I remember Grandma saying, "We thought of doing something, but we had to choose, and we chose to spend our money and time on refurbishing the house, which was in a terrible state."' Their priority was installing decent water and heating systems. They did, however, remove inappropriate Victorian parterres from the front of the house and created a fine pleached-lime plantation linking the house and the stables.

During Sybil's lifetime the walled garden had been mostly grassed over, with a few cutting beds and some fruit and vegetables, and it needed attention. So, a couple of years after her death, Cholmondeley set about creating a new garden in her memory; this opened to the public in 1996.

Five acres is a lot of flat space to fill – the garden probably originally contained kennels, which would account for its size – so the first thing was to divide it up with yew hedges, 'rather like Sissinghurst', Cholmondeley says. 'The garden is four walls and no features. It all has to be in the planting.'

The space is laid out on a formal grid of discrete areas or 'rooms', with different interest and moods. There is an Italian enclosure, with box parterres; a formal rose garden, dotted with statues and based on one of the William Kent ceilings in the house; a French garden of pleached limes and plum trees, underplanted with spring bulbs; and a croquet lawn. The hedges, some cut in swags, give height and form, teasing you into exploring round the corner.

Paul Underwood and Simon Martin, the gardeners who laid out the plans, have since moved on, and there is now a full-time team of two, led by Mhari Blanchfield, with four part-timers.

Julian and Isabel Bannerman, whose work Cholmondeley had seen at Waddesdon Manor, in Buckinghamshire, and Highgrove, the Prince of Wales's house in Gloucestershire, were brought in as consultants to design some of the hard landscaping and borders in 1999. 'We needed new ideas and knowledge,' Cholmondeley recalls.

The Bannermans built the rustic temple pavilion, which is the focal point at the end of a 120-foot double border running down the centre of the garden, moving colourwise from cool to hot. They also designed a large oak-beamed fruit cage housing cherries, kiwi fruits, currants and red and white gooseberries; it is modelled on one of the turrets in the stable block next door.

The formality is in accord with the house, built in the 1720s on the site of an older property, by Robert Walpole, effectively Britain's first prime minister, who made a fortune at an early age and became the first Earl of Orford. It was designed by James Gibbs and Colen Campbell, with interiors by William Kent, to a grand plan that, says Cholmondeley, 'was built to impress and to show Walpole was as good as any duke.' His political enemies, however, 'thought it was terribly vulgar and over the top: too much gilding.'

Inherited by the Cholmondeley family through marriage in 1797, Houghton Hall is surrounded by a thousand acres of parkland grazed by white fallow deer, the antlers of which decorate the pavilion. It has thirteen bedrooms, along with several state apartments adorned with precious eighteenth-century fabrics. They are never used, but are open to the public. 'I don't know who slept there last,' Cholmondeley says. 'Probably George IV, who said he had never spent a worse night. Maybe he saw something unpleasant – we always thought that particular room was very spooky.' From about 1880, the estate was rented out; it was popular with tenants who indulged in the cull-like shoots that Edward VII made popular at Sandringham, next door. 'We have pictures of him sitting there surrounded by thousands of birds.' It was after the First World War that

Lord Cholmondeley, in the walled garden created in honour of his grandmother, Sybil Sassoon.

the future 5th Marquess and Sybil, his wife, came to live at Houghton and set about restoring the estate.

In one of the 'rooms' in the walled garden, a new sculpture by the Danish artist Jeppe Hein is being installed, surrounded by laburnum bushes and irises, which will have a short but brilliant season of colour for just three or four weeks in early summer. The sculpture, however, which consists of a jet of water surmounted by a ball of flame, should intrigue visitors throughout the year. 'I hope it will be good fun,' Cholmondeley says.

This is the first sculpture within the walls, but the eighteenth-century parkland, designed by Charles Bridgeman, already houses several contemporary pieces. To the east of the house is a circle of Cornish slate at the end of a path mown through the grass. Designed by Richard Long, it is one of the works that Cholmondeley has commissioned for Houghton. He has the space and the money to let artists do what they want. 'If you can do that with artists, it's great fun, and nice for them, too.'

In a wooded area to the side of the west front are two modern follies. The first is Skyspace, by the American artist James Turrell: an oak-clad building raised on stilts, in which you sit and contemplate the sky through the open roof. (It is more interesting than it sounds.) The other, by Stephen Cox, is a sarcophagus-like marble structure sitting at the end of a path and in the dappled shade of the trees around. Nearby is a copper beech hedge by Anya Gallaccio, based on Sybil's signature. When it has grown to full height, Cholmondeley jokes, you might need a helicopter to see it to full effect.

As well as creating the new garden, Cholmondeley has been working to restore the park to its original splendour. This includes re-installing Bridgeman's eighteenth-century semicircular ha-ha in place of the barbed-wire fence he remembers from his childhood, beyond which were fields of sugar beet. Now the beet has gone, and in its place is a wide grassy avenue, with woodland to either side. Lining the edges, double allées of lime have been planted, giving the woodland almost two miles of bright green fringes when in leaf. The wildernesses of shrubs and trees nearer the house are also being replanted, to an eighteenth-century plan.

It may not be as dramatic a change as in the walled garden, but, as Walpole's youngest son, Horace, wrote of William Kent in his celebrated 1780 essay 'On Modern Gardening': 'He leaped the fence, and saw that all nature was a garden.'

11 May 2008

Lord Cholmondeley married Rose Hanbury in 2009 and they live at Houghton along with their twin boys, Xan and Ollie, and daughter, Iris. He is still adding to the sculpture collection.

Antlers shed by the white fallow deer in Houghton's parkland adorn the pediment of the Bannermans' rustic oak temple.

The Chiral Terrace explores the right- and left-handed nature of molecules.

CHRISTINE FACER

Gloucestershire

Gardens, for most of us, are about creating a space in which to relax and admire the glories of nature. There is, however, a tradition, stretching back to the Greeks and Romans, in which the landscape is for serious contemplation and allusion to philosophy, religion, politics and the classics.

The three acres of gardens at Througham Court, Christine Facer's seventeenth-century manor near Stroud, in Gloucestershire, are firmly in this metaphorical tradition, but her points of reference are scientific – considering such weighty matters as chaos theory, the evolution of the universe and chirality (in chemistry, the 'left- or right-handed nature' of molecules, for example in our bodies or in drugs). 'Science provides the new metaphors for the new century,' says Facer. 'It is so interesting, it is so sexy – so why not put it in the garden?'

In her fifties, with blonde hair and a petite figure, Facer is in the Baroness Susan Greenfield school of sexy scientists. An expert in malaria, she was a reader in tropical haematology at the Royal London Hospital before retraining as a landscape designer in 1999. Her hero is Charles Jencks, whose thirty-acre Garden of Cosmic Speculation at Portrack, in Dumfries and Galloway, tackles similar matters of the universe.

There are plenty of brainy designers working in Britain today, but – Portrack and a few others apart – there is a shortage of gardens that overtly express their intellectuality. Gardens based largely on ideas have been slow to catch the public imagination. Througham Court is an exception: here, traditional and cutting-edge, challenging design sit happily side by side. Facer, who created a Genetic Garden at the Westonbirt garden festival in 2002, uses it to show clients her work. She and her husband, judge Anthony Hoffman, bought the house in 1995 and inherited a garden designed by Norman Jewson, an early-twentieth-century Arts and Crafts architect who also did some work on the house. Jewson's client was Michael Sadleir, the author of *Fanny by Gaslight*, a 1940 tale of Victorian prostitution that was made into a film starring James Mason and Phyllis Calvert.

Facer has kept much of his work, including a sunken parterre (though she has modernized the planting within the box hedges), an Italian garden and topiary yews – once sculpted into birds, but now in more 'interesting' forms. Her latest addition is the striking Chiral Terrace: large diamond-shaped slabs of black granite, white limestone and red acrylic, enclosed by a ring of polished stainless steel. A rill filled with (non-toxic) black-dyed water reflects a stone inscribed with the word 'chirality' and various mirror-image chemical formulas are carved into stones. The terrace is as much a feat of technical skill as a thought-provoking work of art, in that each heavy piece had to be cut exactly and fitted together.

Six out of six: sandstone balls sit on mirrors reflecting the skies, and represent the six numbers that govern the expansion of the universe.

The formulae and clever visual puns are a lot to take in if you are not scientifically informed, but Facer is determined that her work should be accessible and read at many levels. 'You don't need a scientific background to appreciate what is going on,' she says. 'Though I think gardens of the twenty-first century should be challenging. They should say: "Look at me. What do you think I am?" If people come away learning something, then that is good. You should push the boundaries.' So, the entry to the vegetable garden could just be a gate with striking brushed-steel panels on it; alternatively, if you are conversant with chaos theory, you would recognize the spiky patterns they display. Likewise, the winding path that has been cut through the meadow is planted with silver birches spaced at distances that accord with the Fibonacci sequence: at one metre apart, then two, then three, then five – each new distance being the sum of the two previous ones.

The pattern, discovered by the thirteenth-century Italian mathematician who lends his name to it, is found widely in nature – in the number of petals on a flower, the bones in your hand and the shape of a snail's shell, for instance. It is also related to the Golden Section followed by architects. 'It is pleasing to the eye,' Facer explains. 'If you do anything out of that proportion, it doesn't look right.'

Fibonacci may have written his sequence more than eight hundred years ago, and inspired the trail through the meadow, but Facer's Cosmic Evolution Garden is based on *Just Six Numbers: the Deep Forces that Shape the Universe* by Martin Rees, the Astronomer Royal, which was published in 2000.

'It is all about the evolution of the universe,' says Facer, as we contemplate six sandstone balls sitting on mirrors that reflect the sky in an area enclosed by high yew hedges. Each is engraved with one of the six numbers that govern the expansion of the universe: from the smallest, epsilon (0.007), the strongest number in the universe, representing nuclear energy, to nu (10 to the 36th power), the largest, relating to the strength of gravity.

That's not to say that Facer's designs are po-faced. In the Cosmic Garden, as well as a seat representing a black hole (it looks as if it is being sucked into the ground), the plants are related to matters stellar and cosmic – the likes of *Cosmos sulphureus* 'Cosmic Orange', *Ligularia stenocephala* 'The Rocket' and *Ophiopogon planiscapus* 'Nigrescens' (representing the blackness of space). To cheer up a shady set of steps that lead to an allée of pleached limes, she has covered them in bright red artificial turf and called them the Royal Steps. A sculpture of library shelves includes a book engraved with Tim Shutter, the maker's name. 'Heavy reading,' she quips, as she picks it up.

One for a pun: Christine Facer.

Facer has converted one of the outbuildings into a reception room, where she plays host to groups visiting the garden. The end wall is glass, and gives wide views over Holy Brook valley, where not another house can be seen.

Close to the window, in a sunny, well-drained spot, is what Facer describes as her 'rusty border', full of golden, purple, burnt-orange and red flowerers such as achillea, eremurus, salvia and dark 'Queen Victoria' lobelia. In the meadow below, which the Fibonacci path cuts through, is a set of fluttering red and purple flags – an ever-changing contrast to the naturalistic landscape as the light moves on through the day.

Whether visitors looking out of the window appreciate the flags breaking up their views over one of the loveliest areas of England is secondary for Facer. The aim is that her work sticks in the mind. A recent visitor told her: 'I can't get your garden out of my head.' 'To me, that is really pleasing,' Facer says. 'That someone has thought about it – and is still thinking about it.'

17 August 2008

Facer is still using the garden as somewhere to explore scientific matters. She writes: 'The garden continues to grow and evolve. Fractal shapes, as seen in the borrowed landscape, have been used to create a portrait in the Fractal Valley Gate. Novel plantings have been introduced and a new design for the garden, in collaboration with Charles Jencks, questions and theorizes the importance of epigenetics as a leading edge in the multifold influences on evolution as conceived today.'

And, if you can't get your head round such complex matters, it remains a beautiful garden, with or without chaos theory thrown in.

JULIAN & ISABEL BANNERMAN

Gloucestershire

Julian Bannerman is trying to balance a golden crown on a fluctuating jet of water, and there is a periodic clunk as it flies off and hits the ground: the filter has blocked up, creating problems with the pressure. It is his new party piece, and marks the end of the route that the public takes round his garden at Hanham Court, near Bristol. Perhaps the blockage is a sign that such an irreverent device equates to *lèse-majesté*: after all, Julian and his wife, Isabel, are garden designers by appointment to HRH the Prince of Wales for their work at Highgrove, Prince Charles's Gloucestershire home.

The Bannermans included a similar 'dancing crown' in the Collector Earl's Garden for the Duchess of Norfolk, at Arundel Castle, in West Sussex, which HRH opened last year with no objection. At Hanham Court, they have combined it with a cascade and pool to disguise an old septic tank, overlooked by a statue of Neptune and surrounded by a stumpery: a Victorian confection of a garden, fashioned from gnarled tree roots.

It was for a similar stumpery – among other work – that they won their endorsement from Prince Charles; their own stumpery is created from sweet chestnuts left over from the Highgrove job, arranged with ferns and holey stones. It is also typical of the Bannermans' style, which combines romantic planting with a spadeful or two of theatricality: many of their gardens are peppered with temples, follies and obelisks, and their gold-medal-winning entry at Chelsea in 1994 featured the ruins of an old abbey. Had life turned out differently for the couple, who have worked together since 1983, they 'would have loved to be architects or stage designers,' says Isabel.

In the formal garden at Hanham Court, there are borders filled with traditional favourites such as roses, philadelphus, irises, peonies, regal lilies and delphiniums, but all is not as straightforward as it might at first appear. The yews planted along borders beside the 'landing strip', as they call the Tudor bowling lawn that runs the length of the garden, have been clipped into cones with rooks' nests of branches on top, which will be worked into topiary shapes when they are big enough. A cartoon-like treehouse peeks out of another yew, this time left to grow into clouds of branches; an obelisk sits in woodland at the end of a path; and by the swimming pool is a columned fountain, its walls lined with tufa and ammonites. The Bannermans use these two materials frequently, cut and chiselled to look like more expensive stone and nodding to the style of Inigo Jones – who was, of course, both architect and stage designer.

Julian and Isabel Bannerman, at the edge of the 'landing strip', a former Tudor bowling lawn.

Their home is on the outskirts of the suburb of Keynsham, but once you've turned down the drive, the twenty-first century seems as far away as the distant roar of the A4; surrounded by fields, the seven-bedroom house sits in its own narrow, sloping valley. The Bannermans have lived here for fifteen years, but only now do they feel ready to let in visitors on a regular basis. 'There comes a time when you have done nearly everything, and it does feel a bit of a shame hiding something so nice,' says Julian. And, after all, £5 a head, plus the proceeds of plant sales and teas, won't go amiss, even for royal designers.

They had a dry run a couple of years ago, opening for a day in June for the National Gardens Scheme. Seven hundred people turned up – not surprising, given that the couple have worked on many of the grandest estates, creating gardens for, among others, the Marquess of Cholmondeley at Houghton Hall, in Norfolk (see page 50); Lord Rothschild at Waddesdon Manor, in Buckinghamshire; and Lord Lloyd-Webber at Sydmonton, in Hampshire. 'It was terrifying,' Julian says. 'All the lanes were blocked.'

Neither Julian nor Isabel gives the impression that much would terrify them. They seem quite at ease with strangers wandering their terraces, which, together with a park and woodland, cover twenty-five acres. 'I'm a bit like Disraeli,' says Julian. 'I like looking at people in my park rather than animals. We only have four sheep.'

The house itself is as romantic as the garden, a pile of many layers that has grown organically until it envelops the walls of the adjoining fourteenth-

The swimming pool, surrounded by pots and romantic 'ruins'.

century church like creeping ivy. Parts were built as a pre-Reformation monastic foundation, others have been 'Georgianified'. A Victorian turret, complete with gargoyles, has been added in a corner, the walls are covered in banksia roses and wisteria, and at the back, where teas are served, is an Arts and Crafts loggia. The formal areas – the lawn, borders, terraces and pool – are on a medieval bastion, which was probably fortified in its early days. It juts out 'like an aircraft carrier' along the length of the valley and covers a nib of rock. Building a wall around the rock and filling in the area with soil has created a level surface.

Below the walls, there is parkland on one side, the last of the Cotswold limestone, and, further down, an orchard filled with old varieties of apples; on the other side is a wooded dell, thick with magnolias, lilac, philadelphus and, rather incongruously, a clump of alien-looking tree ferns by a shady pool.

When the couple bought the house from a Bristol pawnbroker, the garden was almost non-existent, serving mainly as a latrine for the resident Great Dane. Isabel was not convinced. 'It was pretty spooky,' she says. So why did they buy it? 'We got a lot of architecture for our money.' And the garden? 'It was overgrown, with sycamore, leylandii and brambles; you couldn't see out at all. Julian thought the topography was amazing, though it was hard to grasp that at the time.'

The garden took a while to take shape, as other matters had priority. 'We had to redo the roof of the house,' Isabel says. 'It was desperate.' They were also busy raising their sons. Ismay, now twenty, Rex, eighteen, and Bertie, fifteen, who

The dancing crown, behaving at last, in the stumpery.

was born three days after they moved in. So, rather than working on the areas around the house, they started under a huge walnut tree in the parkland. 'We knew we wanted to do a lot to the main garden, but we didn't have the money, so it was easier just to plant some bulbs.' In spring, it is a sea of snowdrops, fritillaries and narcissus.

The next few weeks of the year are Julian's favourite time, when the roses start to bloom. 'It is all full of promise, a bit like the start of a marriage,' he says.

Their aim, Julian explains, is to 'do a Christopher Lloyd' – introduce more exotic reds, purples and golds, as used in Lloyd's garden at Great Dixter, in Sussex. So they are planting seven thousand nasturtiums, *Helenium* 'Moorheim Beauty', cannas, crocosmias and datura. 'It is going to be our real challenge,' says Julian, adding, with an uncharacteristic lack of confidence: 'We are probably going to screw up.' That would be unlikely.

31 May 2009

The Bannermans sold Hanham Court in 2011 and moved to Trematon Castle in Cornwall, where they have made a gloriously romantic garden.

WILL ALSOP

Norfolk

Will Alsop OBE, the maverick architect and member of the Royal Academy (he is one of the selectors of this year's Summer Exhibition), has won many awards over his sixty-one years. There is one, however, that has so far eluded him: best front garden of the year in Sheringham, north Norfolk, where he and his wife, Sheila, have had a holiday home for more than twenty-five years. 'It would mean more to me than the Stirling prize.'

Alsop is best known for modernist buildings such as Peckham Library, in south London, where the upper floors are supported on spindly legs that look like skew-whiff knitting needles – for which he bagged the said Stirling prize in 2000. One of his most high-profile works in progress is Chips, a residential building in Manchester that does indeed resemble a neatly stacked pile of *pommes frites*.

So, it is something of a surprise to walk down the stone-set path of the long front garden in Norfolk, under the shade of a Giverny-style arbour, and arrive at a late-Victorian red-brick house filled with comfortable sofas, books, antique china and paintings. Where are the contemporary building materials, the modernist furniture, the wacky colours?

'It's not just my house, it's Sheila's as well. I concur with her taste,' says the man sometimes known as Mr Blobby – surely for the splashes of colour on his buildings, rather than his cheerfully unkempt appearance, which comes wreathed in a fug of cigarette smoke. 'This is not great art; the house has nothing to do with great design. Using a word that most architects don't use, it is "cosy", and I am comfortable with that. Actually, as I get older, I try to incorporate that in my other work.'

We sit in the glass- and aluminium-walled dining room that Alsop added to the back of the house with materials left over from a project in France. The room, which replaced a conservatory and small terrace, is contemporary in feel, but hardly pushes the frontiers of design. Beneath, in a series of terraces, is a narrow jungle of a garden, planted with tree ferns, phormiums, palms and large pots of hostas and hydrangeas. You can just see the sea through the trees and over the top of the boundary wall. Goldfish swim in the small pond beneath the window.

There's a lunchtime bottle of red (actually, it is rather before lunchtime) on the long maple table, which Alsop designed. He points to a sofa at the end of the room that catches the evening light. 'If you really analyse both the house and garden, it is all about different places to sit,' he says. 'I like a bit of sitting. That's the gin-and-tonic sofa.'

Another favourite G&T spot is an outdoor bench by the front door, which benefits from the warmth captured by the red-brick wall behind it. Similar seats are dotted around the jungly garden for different parts of the day. There is even one by the barbecue, though, he says, 'We try not to have barbecues – dangerous things. They are the quickest way to arguments.'

The Alsops bought the five-bedroom house in 1982, as they wanted somewhere out of London for weekends and holidays. The country breaks come less frequently nowadays, as Alsop is often abroad on business; he has offices in Shanghai, Beijing, Toronto and Singapore, and is a professor of architecture in Vienna.

Sheila's parents lived nearby and the house is also a six-minute walk from the station, which was convenient, as Sheila didn't drive at the time. When their children, Oliver, Nancy and Piers, were growing up, friends could easily be collected from the station.

Queen Victoria's visits to the nearby Sandringham estate, which she bought in 1863, popularized the area, but Sheringham is now

Will Alsop, on the way to find somewhere to sit in his garden.

a rather old-fashioned kind of seaside resort. The town has several run-down hotels, a legacy from its Victorian glory days. 'If someone wanted to invest, you could do something fantastic with these hotels, but they don't, so that's the end of it,' says Alsop. His own house was once the stables for such a hotel. In the Second World War, it was used by the military for maintaining motor vehicles. A local builder converted it in 1951, and it was pretty much unchanged when the Alsops bought it thirty years later from the estate of an old lady who had died some time before. 'The house had been empty for six or nine months. Houses show that; you feel it when you go into them.'

Just as he was unpacking the furniture, Alsop got a phone call. 'This is really peculiar. It was North Norfolk district council, wanting me to build a swimming pool in Sheringham. I thought it was my business partner [at the time, John Lyall] playing a joke on me. In the end, I said, "F*** off, John" – but then I realized it was a genuine inquiry.' Alsop's unorthodox response to his first stand-alone commission didn't deter the council, and the pool, finished in 1987 and opened

Tree ferns and palms help to create a jungly atmosphere behind the glass extension.

by Princess Diana, still exists. 'Except that they have ruined it,' he laments. 'They have painted the outside blue and yellow to cheer it up. It is supposed to be stained timber.'

The project was a good way to spend time in the town and get to know it. 'I started to fiddle with the house, a bit here, a bit there; it just evolved.' As did the garden, which grew over the years from a narrow strip at the back of the house to encompass two extra areas bought from neighbours around the corner – visitors liken it to a Tardis.

'I would plant a few things, then come back, and suddenly they were in flower. You get this delayed joy; that is terrific. From that, I became more and more serious, and started to think about what I would like it to be.'

At the far end is Alsop's studio, next to a paved patio with yet more seating. On the table is a thick pile of his paintings. He has one in the Royal Academy's summer show of some flower-like shapes. Its title? *I Wish My Garden Was Really*

Like This. In fact, the garden at the back of the house is more about greenery and strong shapes than a riot of floral abundance. He and Sheila 'don't go for lots of colour.'

Thanks to the mild seaside climate, they have pines, figs, a tamarisk, South African restios, potted shrubs and ivy-clad walls. A canopy of high branches covers much of the space in dappled shade. 'It's a high umbrella and a garden full of telegraph poles,' he jokes. Perhaps his garden is where he got his inspiration for Peckham Library.

The front garden is more formal, with a series of parallel lines created by the path, a long rectangular pond (or 'short canal', as Sheila calls it) and a row of agaves in long-tom pots. Extending down the garden is a box parterre, in which olive trees are planted. There is also an Indian chestnut tree near the street. Alsop had hoped its black nuts would be his secret weapon in the annual office conker championships. 'They are not. They are pathetic.'

Away from the front garden's formal structure, things are left pretty much to themselves. At this time of year, self-seeded hollyhocks and campanulas are happily flowering beneath the arbour and in the gravel beside it. 'An over-designed garden feels dead,' says Alsop.

His approach to his outdoor space is much the same as to his architecture – letting the other elements, whether they are plants, clients or local communities, play their part, and not being too precious about allowing their contributions. 'In your twenties, you think reading the philosophers and indulging in theory is going to help,' he explains. 'I can assure you that it doesn't. By the time you get to your thirties, you downgrade it all to "concept". At forty, that becomes, "Well, maybe the idea is all right." At fifty, it's "a notion". At sixty, "Not a f***ing clue."

'It's sort of liberating. I have become suspicious, whether it is a garden or whatever, when people start talking about the justification for their design. I don't believe in the word "inspiration". You just have to do it.'

21 June 2009

Sheila has since decided that the 'short canal' was bad feng shui (this has coincided with the arrival of grandchildren), so Alsop has made it into a bog garden, filled with gunnera and bulrushes and is trying to encourage roses to flower high above the box hedge to create 'flying colour'. In the back garden, he has added echiums – 'they are quite prehistoric'– and the view from the dining room is now even more jungly, creating an Alsopian microcosm hidden from the other houses. 'It keeps me happy.'

SHIRLEY SHERWOOD

Oxfordshire

It's easy to imagine contemporary botanical artists standing to attention, their hair brushed and shoes polished, when Dr Shirley Sherwood decides to take a look at their work. As the owner of more than seven hundred paintings, she is the world's leading collector of the genre (she leaves pre-twentieth-century art to others) and has done more than anyone else to elevate the status of those who painstakingly – and often beautifully – record our plants in minute detail.

'I could be modest and say no, but that just isn't true,' says Sherwood, as we inspect works at Hinton Manor – her country pile near Faringdon, Oxfordshire – by the likes of Rory McEwen, a Scottish artist painting on vellum; Margaret Mee, the British artist who was one of the first to bring the plight of the Brazilian rainforests to the world's attention in the 1950s; and Paul Jones, from Australia, whose works are also collected by the Ashmolean Museum in Oxford and the Smithsonian in Washington, DC.

The earliest in the collection is dated 1947, though most have been painted in the past fifteen years, many of them commissioned by Sherwood. 'I have actually changed the whole concept,' she says. 'It is very interesting that one person can do this. I never intended to, it wasn't my plan at all.'

Sherwood has had a lifelong passion for plants. She read botany at Oxford in the 1950s, before moving into pharmacological research. She has long admired botanical art and considered taking it up herself before concluding it would take her too long to reach a high enough standard. So she decided to collect instead. Her first purchase, in 1990, was a depiction of a pink orchid by Pandora Sellars, a leading contemporary artist, which she bought for £3,330.

'There's some wonderful stuff out there,' she says. 'It is vastly underrated. I have works by 241 artists from all around the world, including China, Japan, Australia, South Africa and South America – it goes on.' About a hundred of them are in the house; the rest are in a studio in her five-acre garden. At present, however, there are a few gaps: more than 130 pictures are hanging in an exhibition, 'The Art of Plant Evolution', in the gallery that bears her name at the Royal Botanic Gardens, Kew. The family gave a generous donation towards the gallery, which opened last year.

Sherwood's American husband, James, founded the shipping company Sea Containers, as well as the Orient Express hotel and train group, from which he

Shirley Sherwood, pictured beside the remains of the moat, which was mentioned in the Domesday Book.

A cedar of Lebanon, surrounded by a host of golden daffodils, near the moat.

stepped down as chairman in 2007. He's not in evidence when I visit the eight-bedroom house, bought more than thirty years ago, where they live when not at their Kensington home or visiting the group's thirty-three hotels around the world.

Parts of the house were built in the fifteenth century, though later additions are Georgian and Victorian. Henry Marten, one of those who signed the death warrant of Charles I, lived there, and Oliver Cromwell is alleged to have stayed there during the Civil War. If you were painting a portrait of the archetypal elegant English country house, complete with a gravel drive that crunches satisfactorily when you walk or drive on it, Hinton Manor would fit the bill. Beside the remnant of a moat mentioned in the Domesday Book (now a long, thin lake) stand three huge cedars of Lebanon that are at least two hundred years old, giving the place a dignified sense of permanence. Sherwood has planted a couple more to take the garden into the next century or two.

Other trees in the parkland beyond were not so hardy. 'When we came here, Dutch elm disease had devastated the place. It was like spillikins,' she says. Now, there are new stands of chestnut, beech, birch, lime and oak, which also filter the wind coming across the fields.

Sherwood has two full-time gardeners to keep the garden looking spick, with another one to cut the grass. Although there is a colourful herbaceous border to

Looking through dangling willows to a new bridge, built for the millennium.

the side of the house, and there are little pockets of surprise – a cottage garden area by the studio, next to a sunny patch planted with desert exotics – much of the garden is devoted to trees and shrubs, many of them unusual. For instance, a swamp cypress stands on the slope below the house, to compliment the equine statue by John Mills, while in the former walled garden she has planted an avenue of *Ginkgo biloba*, one of the world's oldest living tree species, which is looking a bit bedraggled. 'It doesn't really work, but I will get it right one day.'

Unlike her husband, who is uninterested in matters horticultural ('It is a disappointment to me; Americans are not brought up in the tradition of gardening'), Sherwood is keen on cultivating her plot and has done much to restore it, as well as planting new areas, including a dell garden by the swimming pool. 'This was just a hollow with a whole lot of dead elms. There wasn't a single flowering plant in it.' There aren't many in action at the moment, although Sherwood's handkerchief tree put on a fine show earlier in the year, as did the magnolias and candelabra primulas.

Strong vistas everywhere make up for any lack of colour: when you are swimming in the pool, the eye travels under the bridge to the moat, and, cleverly, the layout gives the impression you are doing your laps in a wild pond. Seated on a stone bench under the giant rhubarb-like leaves of a gunnera, you catch a perfectly framed picture, through the branches of a willow, of another bridge to the left, built for the millennium. 'It is a very heavy stone seat,' Sherwood says, which is important: 'The gunnera would just pick a wooden seat out of the way.'

The shade provided by the gunnera is essential for Sherwood. Last year, she only managed to get outside three times, as she has lupus, an autoimmune disease that affects connective tissue and in which the skin can develop a rash if exposed to the sun. It would explain why she is wearing a large hat, sunglasses and baggy clothing when we walk at a sedate pace round the garden and sit in the plant-filled 1830 conservatory, even though the day is overcast.

'I have to cover myself up completely; it's like wearing deep-sea diving gear,' she says. 'It is a very nasty disease and makes you feel exhausted.' Some of the steroids she had to take caused her vertebrae to crumble last year, although she is on a new drug and things are looking up: 'I am walking around quite strongly now.'

It would seem apt that Sherwood has been a medical guinea pig: in the 1970s she was part of the team led by James Black that developed Tagamet, used to treat duodenal ulcers. 'At one time, it was by far the most successful drug in the world and the most profitable; it treated millions of people. Now, Viagra has taken over.'

Having seen Tagamet through to the market, and with two sons from a previous marriage (her first husband died in a plane crash), she married James Sherwood in 1977. Rather than rest on being a rich man's wife, she founded the Orient Express group's magazine, of which she was editor-in-chief for twenty-four years, writing and photographing for it before retiring last year. As well as the famous train, the group owns some of the world's smartest hotels, including Reid's Palace, in Madeira, the Cipriani, in Venice, and the Copacabana Palace, in Rio de Janeiro. Sherwood takes a keen interest in the properties' gardens. 'I just advise a bit; I don't do much,' she says, though one suspects that the gardeners ignore her input at their peril.

Illness and advancing years don't seem to be slowing her down. She's just written a book to accompany the exhibition and has been arguing with Kew about the colour of its cover. 'I like red,' she says. 'If you look at a bookcase, the reds always stand out.' Red it is, then.

30 August 2009

An equestrian sculpture by John Mills makes a striking focal point in the snow. Behind is a young *Cedrus deodara*,

Dr Sherwood has further developed the millennium project at Hinton Manor and has also cut a path up a mound created by the original spoil from the moat. It gives beautiful views of the garden and the Thames.

Her collection of botanical paintings has grown considerably and she continues to mount major shows at the Shirley Sherwood Gallery of Botanical Art in Kew Gardens.

ANDY HULME

London

There's something of Mellors about Andy Hulme. While there is no suggestion that his employer, the fashion designer Vivienne Westwood, has anything other than a happily platonic relationship with her gardener, his thick head of hair and careless stubble, not to mention his penchant for tweed, a roll-up and a good pair of stout boots, exude an air of Lady Chatterley's lover earthiness mixed with a trowelful or two of dandification.

Indeed, so inspired was Westwood by his 'look', she designed her present menswear collection as a homage, and he was among those modelling it on the Milan catwalks in March. 'I'm Vivienne's muse,' he says, obviously tickled by such an honour. He returns the compliment by wearing her creations, even when digging his borders.

'English eccentric' would be another label fit for Hulme. When we meet at his 'garden' in Southwark, south London, he is funny, sunny and charming, if difficult to pin down when it comes to providing actual facts. Perhaps this is something to do with the hangover he is nursing, but to judge by previous phone conversations, his elliptical mode of speech would seem to be the norm.

We sit on a makeshift bench by a high brick wall in what is effectively a guerrilla garden, created on unused land. In front of us is a concreted area owned by Transport for London, about two acres in all, with a railway bridge traversing the far side. Hulme's half-acre territory is tucked into the southern, sunniest corner and sealed off by a high steel fence from the rest, which is used as a car park for Borough food market from Thursday to Saturday. In one corner is an empty static caravan, almost hidden by buddleia and goat willow. Big plastic butts collect rainwater beside it, and compost bins made from pallets line the west wall. With all that concrete around, it can get pretty hot.

Hulme first came here as a security guard in 2005, and lived in the caravan. He now lives in Vauxhall and Northampton, but visits a couple of times a week. 'The whole thing kicked off when I was in an extreme state of grief. A friend, Mark Blanco, had died [he fell off a balcony at a party in December 2006 in mysterious circumstances, aged thirty]. He was an activist, an intellectual and a gentleman. It's a memorial to him and to the future.'

Hulme, along with Sidney Dacres, a Jamaican-born farmer, has created a space that would make Blanco proud. In early summer, it is a sea of opium poppies;

Andy Hulme, dapperly dressed, with his foot resting on the pyramid made from rubble and old bones.

A photograph of the garden in its summer glory was – like Hulme – difficult to pin down; this one, however, gives a hint of its eccentric style.

later, evening primroses, mallows, hollyhocks, sunflowers and field poppies take over. Agapanthus, nasturtiums, self-seeded fennel and a crab apple are also among the plants, creating a wonderfully tuneful chaos. Specimens such as a camellia and a heart-shaped privet topiary bush ('It was a globe, but it started to get a bit mouldy underneath, so I trimmed it') have come from previous garden jobs, although Hulme is a bit vague as to which ones – perhaps in case the garden owners want them back.

By tradition, the site is known as an ancient graveyard for prostitutes, who were excluded from being interred alongside more godly folk; in the fourteenth century it was recorded as an unconsecrated burial ground for 'single women'. Later, it became a general paupers' graveyard before being closed in 1853, too full to take any more.

When Hulme arrived, the site was 'just rubble, walls, brick dust and crushed asbestos'. That the plants have somewhere to root is due to him importing sacks of soil, again a by-product of jobs he has worked on. 'For a while, everyone wanted sunken gardens and ponds.' The rubble was the result of excavation for a dig by the Museum of London between 1992 and 1998, during work on the Jubilee line extension.

The rubble has been put to good use as walls to hold in the imported soil, and Hulme and Dacres also piled it high into a pyramid. 'It was a way to get rid of it,' Hulme admits, although it also makes a seemly focal point for the garden. If you look closely enough at the lumps, you can spot bits of bone in the concrete.

Down by the fence is an area rather different in style: a statue of the Virgin Mary – or another saintly woman, it's difficult to tell – with candles around it, like a shrine, and potted plants that would be more at home on a patio than with Hulme's anarchic style. Tied to the iron railings of a gate are talismans and ribbons bearing the names of 'fallen women' through the ages. This is the work of a group called Crossbones, which every year holds a candlelit Halloween procession to the site. Its leader is John Constable, whose alter ego, the poet and shaman John Crow, is inspired by the spirit of a medieval Bankside whore.

One gets the feeling that Hulme finds the group's decoration of the site and planting scheme not entirely to his taste, but he is an easy-going chap and sees that they have as much right to be there as he has: 'I do my thing and they do theirs.' Crossbones is now lobbying to make the site a permanent memorial to those buried there, and to sex workers in general.

As for Hulme and his own relationship with what he has created, he realizes that it is not going to be permanent. Indeed, its ephemeral nature appeals to him. 'I'm just using it while nobody else is,' he says. 'The dead people, I know, would want to see something cheerful.'

20 September 2009

Andy Hulme left the garden a few years ago and says, 'I don't think about it.' It has now been re-landscaped and Crossbones Garden of Remembrance is open to the public.

Bob Flowerdew
Norfolk

If you ask gardeners in this country why they cultivate their tilth, most will say it is to create somewhere beautiful in which they and their family can spend time relaxing. Over the past few years, growing your own food has become important, but, ultimately, producing pretty plants – edible or not – is still going to come out top of the polls.

For Bob Flowerdew, however, the beauty is all in the bite. His garden in Dickleburgh, near Diss, Norfolk, is a huge testing ground for the best produce for his family's plates, and those of the 920,000 listeners to BBC Radio 4's *Gardeners' Question Time*, on which he has been a panellist for seventeen years. His recommendations of the tastiest tomatoes for outdoor cultivation or how to grow pineapples are as much part of the middle-class aural wallpaper as Ruth and David Archer squabbling in the cowshed.

Flowerdew has lived in his three-bedroom bungalow for twenty-six years. He now shares it with his Jamaican-born wife, Vonnetta, whom he married in 2002, and their four-year-old twins, Malachi and Italia. Although he writes prolifically – his books on organic gardening have sold more than five hundred thousand copies – he keeps a low profile. 'Well, I'm not trying to be a celebrity,' he says. 'I'm trying to remain an expert.'

Interviewing Flowerdew – and yes, that is his real name; the family has been in the county for at least five hundred years – is like a one-on-one *Gardeners' Question Time*. The man hardly draws breath, cheerfully dispensing horticultural tips as if he were giving away free packets of lettuce seed.

It is not that he is pompous, just that he can't help talking about the thing he loves. And he is certainly not fussy about looking smart: on a chilly day, he flings on one of his wife's cardigans and slips wellies over his bobbly old tracksuit pants. Were it not for his trademark waist-length plait, you would suspect him of caring not a sun-ripened fig for appearances. 'My wife says, "Will you please look in a mirror? You've got mud all over your face."'

The garden, covering three-quarters of an acre, is, basically, a giant allotment that produces year-round organic food for the family. Ornamental plants hardly get a look-in. Nor does Vonnetta, so it is a good thing she doesn't want to join him in the veg beds. 'My previous girlfriend loved gardening. The trouble is, she wanted to take over,' he jokes. 'It wasn't my garden any more.' The battle between the sexes over the beds is an issue that often comes up on *Gardeners' Question Time*. 'The answer is: find a partner who doesn't like gardening. A plane can only have one pilot.'

Bob Flowerdew, demonstrating how many apples can be stored in an old chest freezer.

We asked Bob to send in some pictures of his garden in its glory. The top one he captioned 'veg beds and staff'; the bottom shows 'Cosmos' potatoes ('the best chipper') growing on an old compost heap.

Judging from Vonnetta's impressive red-painted talons and the gorgeous high-heeled shoes stacked in the hallway, if she were to take over the cockpit, the garden would have more emphasis on beautiful borders. As it is, Flowerdew is more concerned with thrift and nutritional value than visuals; his is no decorative, Villandry-style potager.

If newspaper makes the best mulch and saves on weeding, he will spread it out on the ground. Piles of old tyres make not only good walls, but also containers in which to grow strawberries. Citrus fruits and tender plants are raised in old plastic buckets that, in winter, can be brought under cover in the large polytunnel. Here the paths are made from old white radiators, laid flat to bounce around the light, and there is another bubble-wrap tent within, providing an inner sanctum in winter for more tender plants, such as sugar cane and pineapples, which are warmed with a 1kW fan heater.

Old chest freezers, with their seals pierced to let in air, make convenient, if not exactly picturesque, storage for apples and pears in the sheds outside, and by an old sofa is a pile of what looks like sheep's wool: in fact, it is Vonnetta's discarded hairpieces, which Flowerdew hangs on lines to scare the birds off his seedlings.

He has recently published the paperback edition of *Grow Your Own, Eat Your Own*, the ingredients of which include growing instructions and recipes, as well as different ways of extending the season by growing under cover and staggering sowing times. When there is a glut, as well as using the freezer, he shows us how to smoke and juice, bottle and jam, pickle and crystallize.

He also wants us to experiment: to nibble away at the fruits of a Swiss cheese plant (the pulp is like a cross between an apple and a banana), the berries of a fuchsia (the 'Californian Dreamers' series and *F. procumbens* have the best flavours), the sweetly fleshy and perfumed strawberry guava, *Psidium cattleianum* (which needs winter protection from frost) and, for the brave, the chokeberry (aronia), full of vitamin C, although that might be a challenge too far in terms of astringency. 'To use the Norfolk, it draws your arse up to your elbow,' says a chortling Flowerdew.

With all this produce, including honey from beehives and meat and eggs from his chickens, you would think he never visits the shops. Not so. 'I spend a fortune,' he confesses. 'The Norfolk catch of anchovies is very light most years, and so is olive oil production. I've had olive trees here for twenty-something years and have only had one olive. It came with the original tree.'

It is refreshing to meet someone so content with what they have, seemingly possessed of a Candide-like appreciation that, in order to be happy, we must cultivate our gardens. As he says on his website: 'I've also played in a local band, sung in a choir, I draw, paint and pastel, and have been hung in Norwich's School of Art, sculpt and carve, cook fabulous food, make the best juices, wines and delights, so live better than a king.'

23 May 2010

Flowerdew is still cultivating his garden in his unique way, although he grows fewer unusual crops and more staples nowadays, in order to feed the family. You can keep up to date with the garden via his Twitter account, @FlowerdewBob, and his website, bobflowerdew.com

JOHN & JENNY MAKEPEACE

Dorset

Chalk and cheese, Venus and Mars: if ever there were a garden that demonstrates archetypal differences between the sexes, it is the one at Farrs, the Dorset home of the furniture-maker John Makepeace and his wife, Jenny.

They moved to the Grade II*, five-bedroom property in the centre of Beaminster in 2001, after twenty-five years at Grade I Parnham House, on the edge of town, where the formal gardens were very much Jenny's domain. John was too busy running his world-famous design school based at the house (whose alumni include Viscount Linley), as well as creating the pieces that earned him an OBE in 1988 for his services to the craft. His first solo exhibition in fifty years of design (he always used to show alongside his students) starts touring this month and it includes chairs, tables and cabinets borrowed from galleries and clients around the world.

While John was beavering away in his workshops, Jenny had her head down in a flower bed. She opened the grounds at Parnham to the public, and they proved as much of an attraction as the interiors of the house, furnished with John's designs. 'John worked from seven or eight in the morning until midnight and never set foot in the garden. It was mine, all mine,' Jenny says, as we talk in the kitchen at Farrs.

John handed over the reins of the school in 2000 and it has since amalgamated with the Architectural Association, while Parnham House is now privately owned. With more time on his hands, he has allowed his designerly eye to wander outdoors into his wife's hitherto unchallenged domain.

Fortunately, Farrs, which is largely Georgian but with parts dating back to the early seventeenth century, came with two acres. So, rather than fight a turf war, the couple decided each would have their own area, uncompromised by the other's input. A neutral 'two men's land' of lawn, specimen trees and shrubs surrounds the house, edged with billowing clipped yews, which have been there since the 1830s and guard its privacy.

Beyond more hedges, the territorial borders are firmly drawn. At the bottom is Jenny's patch, containing a large glasshouse, a riven-oak-framed fruit cage and an enchanting strawbale building, which serves as her retreat and wears a shaggy toupee of *Clematis* 'Broughton Star'. It is also a riot of colour, romance and planned chaos, with raised beds spilling over with flowers, fruit and vegetables. Dahlias in wines, golds and tangerine; gaura, sweet peas, penstemons, verbena, lilies, gladioli, eryngium: all are planted with an abandon that actually needs a painterly skill to achieve.

'At Parnham, I had fourteen acres to play with,' she says. 'Here I can't buy a single plant without thinking about where I'm going to put it.' Conversely, she

John and Jenny Makepeace, together in 'two men's land'. Jenny is sitting on a prototype of a Makepeace 'Innes' chair, made in 1993 from English yew and cast aluminium.

The abundant kitchen garden in Jenny's territory makes a good backdrop for her art.

says, 'If something isn't paying its way, it's gone.' Self-seeders such as eryngium and nigella colonize the gravel paths. That is, all but one, as John has insisted he should have a clear run for his wheelbarrow to reach the compost heap.

Go through an arch in the high hedge and you enter John's world of strong architectural shapes, discipline and greenery. No self-seeders dare march out of rank here. Instead, there are neatly laid blocks restricted to grasses and phormiums. An arching bridge, with a complicated curve designed by John, provides a dash of racy pink in its painted, supporting steel-box beam. It stretches across a water-lily pond to a garden house, furnished only with a sofa and a large sculpture by Tony Heywood.

Rather than letting nature take the upper hand, as his wife has largely done, John's area is all about design, with the plants introduced as instruments to achieve his scheme. After showing little interest in the things over the past twenty-five years, he started mugging up with a vengeance, visiting nurseries and buying single specimens in order to see how they behave. He then worked out where they would go in the third of an acre he can call his own. Those that passed muster included more than thirty varieties of grasses and five of phormiums, including 'Dark Delight' and 'Tricolor'.

Although the hues range from silvery blues through reds to browns, colour takes second place to shape. 'I have limited the plants to those that have strong architectural form,' he says. 'They are part of the design and have to be really quite bold.' They are also expected not to collapse in a soggy heap when battered by wind and rain, which is one of the drawbacks of many grasses. 'I did make one

A curving bridge edged with pink provides a flash of colour in John's grassy domain.

big mistake,' he concedes. 'I thought *Calamagrostis erecta* was going to be more erect.' He had to replace forty plants with 'Karl Foerster', which does the job.

While Jenny's beds are all on a flat plane, John has created hillocks and dips, two terraces and the pond. 'The plan was to break into three dimensions,' he says. The different levels mean the plants can be seen from several heights and angles. Even the sunshade on one of the two terraces fits into the scheme and took some time to find. Most parasols are octagonal, but the paving is laid out in a hexagonal design: to go with that, he eventually settled on a triangular sailcloth, suspended on steel poles.

It was actually Jenny who suggested her husband concentrate on grasses when he was thinking of getting more involved in the garden. She slightly regrets it now and is forever trying to get him to introduce other plants – at the very least, some spring bulbs to cheer things up when the herbaceous varieties have been cut back. 'I might concede to that over time, but I don't want to compromise,' John says, not entirely convinced. 'It would have to be done quite boldly.'

5 September 2010

The Makepeaces continue to garden separately. John reports that Jenny works hard to make her patch ever more colourful, while his grasses 'look great through the winter months, especially on frosty mornings, when traditional gardens don't offer much delight.'

Jilly Cooper I

Gloucestershire

Despite the signs on the front door saying 'Go away' and 'Gone to the pub', and despite being knackered from broken nights – her husband, Leo, has Parkinson's disease and she has been whizzing around the country publicizing her latest novel – Jilly Cooper is doing her best to make Adrian, the photographer, and me welcome in her large Gloucestershire garden.

Adrian's attempts to take a thoughtful portrait of the author are being thwarted as Cooper is constantly throwing her head back in gappy-toothed laughter whenever anyone (including herself) says anything faintly amusing. William, a stout husky/collie melange, is also insisting on being in every picture, while his more picturesque companion, Feather, a greyhound, disdains to play along.

Cooper admires my skirt and moves on to Adrian's shirt. Actually, now she is admiring Adrian himself: 'You look very hunky,' she says. 'I like hunky men.' We are here to look round the garden, but somehow the conversation keeps on veering away from the subject in hand.

'Mellors was a chauffeur, wasn't he?' she goes on (gamekeeper, actually, as she remembers a split second later, but you can see where her mind is going), and this segues into discussing the steeply sloped woodland behind. When Cooper and Leo bought the ten-bedroom, fourteenth-century Cotswold stone house in Bisley in October 1982 they had no idea the eight-acre wood would burst into a haze of bluebells straight out of *Lady Chatterley* the next May.

Cooper's bonkbusters are as thumbed-through for their dirty bits as the books of D.H. Lawrence, albeit written with considerably less of a po face. However, in her latest work, *Jump!*, set in the racy world of racing, the filth is mainly to be found under the fingernails of Etta, the sixty-something heroine. A crush or two aside, what gets her in a lather is to be down on her hands and knees in the border with a trowel, or watching as her beloved horse, Mrs Wilkinson, gallops round the racetrack. This has not stopped the book from selling more than sixty thousand copies in hardback since it was published last month. Etta does eventually get her own roll in the bluebells, but there are a lot of boozy visits to the races and walks with the dogs to go first.

Although the breeches stay more fastened than in works such as *Riders* (1985) and *Polo* (1991), which made her a world bestseller, Cooper has not lost her penchant for a smutty joke, sniggering like a teenage boy as we talk about plants that are good for bedding in up against the wall.

The Coopers bought their first family house in Fulham in 1968. The little garden, however, was little loved. Going through a phase of eating a lot of

Chinese takeaways, 'we'd get drunk and throw the bones into it; we called it the Valley of the Bones,' she confesses.

They then moved west to a house with a bigger garden in Putney, where she became more interested in plants – mostly roses in the 'wrong shade of purple' – using the family allowance for their two adopted children, Felix and Emily, to pay for a gardener. Meanwhile, she got on with her career as a novelist and a columnist for *The Sunday Times*.

In the early 1980s they decided to move to Gloucestershire. 'Someone said they had seen this house on the market. I was brought up in the country and always had visions of myself knee-deep in cow parsley,' says Cooper. What she got instead was 'nettles knocking on each window; I thought, "God, what have I done?"' One of the attractions of the fourteen-acre property, however, was its total privacy. In summer days gone by, she would type her novels in the nude

William the husky/collie cross muscles in on the photograph of Jilly by the pond.

Jilly – and William, again – by one of her long herbaceous borders.

on the terrace so she would get a good all-over tan; these days she merely goes topless. 'Soon I will be too ashamed to do even that.'

On the terrace today are pots of geraniums, adding a 'splash of colour' – a phrase Cooper uses in *Jump!* to describe, with some disdain, the sort of garden crammed with bedding plants and hanging baskets in lurid shades (actually, many a stable yard and racecourse enclosure is guilty). She worries about what is considered acceptable in smart Gloucestershire. 'When I first arrived, my lovely neighbour – she's now dead – said, "My dear, you can't have red in a Cotswold garden." There was a huge red hot poker, so I had to stand in front of it.'

Cooper makes no claim to be a serious gardener, though I suspect she knows more than she is letting on – those long, wide herbaceous borders and specimen trees didn't emerge from nowhere – and she says her recent role has been confined to watering, as she has struggled to produce the novel over the past four years. With her eye off the ball, the gardener has even managed to sneak in the occasional cheery (red) bedder in pots and troughs around the house.

It must be exhausting living in such a critical county. 'Will you tell me what your take is on buddleia?' she asks, sounding as if the gardener is standing by with a saw should I come up with the wrong answer. 'Anna, my PA, says it is very vulgar. I don't think so at all; it has a lovely sweet tobacco scent and reminds me of my darling father, and the butterflies adore it.'

In fact, at this time of year, the garden could do with a splash or two more of colour (though I'm not sure if the fashionable late-season oranges and lipstick pinks would pass the Cotswolds taste test). There are Japanese anemones, echinops and a few roses still in flower in the herbaceous border that runs along the lower terrace, and the trees are turning to their autumnal hues.

The garden's glory day is earlier in the year, when, after drifts of spring bulbs, the clematis and the climbing roses which run rampant through the giant yews are in bloom and the border is full of soft pinks, purples and whites. 'It's not nearly as muted as it should be; there's a lot of very bright phlox and monkshood, and lots of hollyhocks. I love hollyhocks.'

Under the drawing-room window, which is almost smothered in jasmine ('what I'm mad about is scent'), a single, small creamy apricot rose is in bloom – *Rosa* 'Jilly Cooper', named after her by Bill LeGrice of Rosebuddies nursery in Norfolk. Around it are masses of love-in-a-mist, an idea she stole from Highgrove, Prince Charles's country home near by. They have rather taken over now, at the expense of the little rose, but there are worse weeds to have.

Dotted around are several pieces of sculpture, including a group of sheep opposite the front door. The Coopers enjoy commissioning young artists, and on a gable end is an imposing depiction in relief of the Annunciation by a young Paul Day, done when he was still at art college in Cheltenham; he went on to make the controversial kissing couple at St Pancras station in London. At Cooper's insistence, he included a greyhound at the angel's feet. There is a second on another wall, rubbing noses with a cat. An elegant unicorn by Hamish Mackie stands on an ivy-covered plinth, perhaps a warning to visiting journalists – in *Score!* (1999), a hackette meets her end spiked on such a statue's horn.

Near the house is a bed of ruby roses given to the Coopers by friends on their ruby wedding. It needs a weed; with only a part-time gardener and a chap who cuts the lawns, some areas were left to their own devices while Jilly concentrated on taking *Jump!* to the finishing line. As we cross the lawn, she addresses the moles that are producing hills there: 'You must reduce your burrowing.' Amused by her pun, she then shows us the pets' graveyard, with headstones for the beloveds that have gone before, and the tiny seventeenth-century gazebo where she writes her books on Monica, her ancient manual typewriter. There are lovely views across the valley, and a clematis has invaded via the half-open window and curled itself around the lamp while she has been off promoting the book.

'I'd love to take a year off and concentrate on making the garden fantastic,' says Cooper. 'It does need a lot of love.' However, Monica beckons, the clematis will be pruned back, and on she ploughs with the next book.

24 October 2010

By 2018 Jump! *had sold more than 350,000 copies worldwide. Cooper has since published* Mount!, *which came out in paperback in February 2017. Leo died in 2013, and William is now interred in Cooper's pets' cemetery.*

Neil Armstrong, on the steps leading up to Tewlwolow Kernow, one of two skyspaces designed by James Turrell at Tremenheere.

NEIL ARMSTRONG

Cornwall

Within twenty minutes of my meeting Neil Armstrong at Tremenheere, the eleven acres of Cornish hillside he has owned since 1997, he is leading me down a pitch-black passage into a former water tank built into the slope. 'It is very scary,' he warns and, although the Penzance GP doesn't quite say, 'but trust me, I'm a doctor', I am beginning to wonder what we are doing here in the darkness.

He tells me it is a work in progress by James Turrell, the great American installation artist, and that I should be seeing dappled light shining through the leaves outside, projected on to the walls. Nothing: the work is not quite as far on as Armstrong had hoped, and I quickly feel my way back out into the sunlight.

Further acquaintance with the charming and distinctly unscary Armstrong dispels any doubts I may have been having – it was just that he wanted to share his enthusiasm about what is being created here. Since buying the steeply sloping valley overlooking St Michael's Mount, he has been planting it and populating it with works by contemporary artists. The result is one of the most exciting new gardens in the country.

With its benign subtropical climate, Cornwall has long had a tradition of adventurous gardens filled with exotic specimens brought back from distant parts of the globe. These were created with the help of armies of staff, however, so why did Armstrong embark on the herculean task of transforming two fields into his own private Eden singlehandedly, when there isn't even a house on the land? (He lives a few miles away.) Why not take up golf or fast cars – a more usual antidote to listening to people's complaints about their bunions? 'I'm a busy doctor, and it seemed like a nice thing to do,' says the quietly spoken Irishman, as if it is the sort of thing anyone with four children and an equally busy GP wife might contemplate. 'You have to do something. It is a hobby that has got completely out of control.'

Inspired by a late friend who had created a 'wonderland' of exotic specimens near Falmouth, Armstrong bought the valley, which was being sold by a fourth-generation farmer who had nobody to hand it on to. Before the farmer's great-grandfather took it on, in the late nineteenth century, it was owned by Tremenheeres for about six hundred years: they had bought it from the monks of St Michael's Mount in 1290. With good soil, two streams and plenty of shelter provided by the established woodland around its edges, it provided the perfect microclimate for the exotic haven Armstrong planned.

Under the canopy of chestnuts and oaks on the lower slopes, which merge into the land owned by his neighbour, you wander along a streamside boardwalk past a jungle of ferns, rhododendron, pseudopanax, weeping New Zealand

Plants from warmer, arid climes thrive on the sunny upper slopes of the garden.

conifer and dicksonia, planted among the native wildflowers. The dappled shade brings instant feelings of restfulness that should be prescribed on the National Health Service. 'I see a lot of troubled people who could do with coming up here,' Armstrong says.

'It is quite tricky to integrate a strange garden like this into the landscape,' he says, so he has kept this woodland edge muted in varying tones of green. 'It becomes slightly more flamboyant as you reach the centre of the garden.' Marrying the two are more than forty varieties of giant palms, as well as bamboos, bananas and tetrapanax.

The mood gets less lush as you head up the slopes and come further into the full sunlight. At the top of the garden, grasses and restios form thick clumps alongside palms and agave, whereas, further down, cycads – one of the oldest forms of plant life – pepper the lower slopes along with succulents such as aeoniums and agaves.

Armstrong is not one for pretty flowers; he favours a rather more structural approach, in which leaves and stems are of primary importance. It is not only the planting that provides sculpture, however; the human hand has created works of art too, in the form of pieces not only by Turrell but also by David Nash and the Japanese artist Kishio Suga. Each piece is designed for its specific spot: 'I am a gardener, but also the curator of the space, so the artwork, the planting and the landscape have to fit together, without one taking away from the others.'

Black Mound, a sculpture made by David Nash from charred oak, sits in the woodland.

Turrell's installations and 'skyspaces' (buildings that focus the attention on the heavens) are sought after around the world. In fact, it was the artist who originally sought out Armstrong and his land as the perfect site for building such a skyspace to celebrate the solar eclipse of 1999, and then decided to make a more permanent structure on the site.

Like the garden, this is still a work in progress, and Armstrong has further plans to make the garden more visitor-friendly, as, 'to do this as a private project would be pretty indulgent.' These include the opening of a tea room next year on a further five acres of land he has bought at the bottom of the hill. He already has a camera obscura created by Billy Wynter, a local artist, from which to take a different perspective on the garden, and is now thinking of adding a treehouse as yet another way to view the landscape he so loves. 'The madness goes on.'

24 July 2011

Tremenheere is now very much a public garden, with a restaurant, a shop, a nursery and a purpose-built gallery. It is also a member of the Great Gardens of Cornwall group. The Turrell works are completed, and there are about sixteen artworks in all, with the land expanded to cover twenty-two acres. Armstrong is still a full-time GP, as is his wife, though the recent arrival of their first grandchild, he says, 'may be a prompt to re-evaluate.'

WILL FISHER

London

Will Fisher's garden in Camberwell, south-east London, presented him with a problem faced by many city dwellers who live in terraced houses or semis: although an impressive 120 feet in length, it is only 19 feet wide.

The shape would be ideal for a game of cricket (though the neighbours might object to the occasional six flying over the wall). An alternative for those not interested in improving their bowling technique is to divide the garden into different areas, making a journey through varied spaces.

This is something Fisher has done with gusto – although it is not until the far end of the garden that you reach the *pièce de résistance*. Beyond a high wall, made with recycled bricks and guarded by wrought-iron gates against his children – Eliza, five, and Monty, two – you enter a courtyard housing three enormous koi carp in a 19-feet-long formal pond, with an antique Italian fountain mounted on the far wall. On either side, two faded blue doors seemingly lead to the parish church; in fact, hidden from view behind the wall is the pump system for the pond.

Fisher searches the brickwork for signs of moss, which will give it a patina of age akin to the *giardini segreti* of grand Italian villas. The courtyard has been here for only five years, so he has a while to wait. He admits that it is 'technically called a folly – I ran out of money by the time I got to the gate. We still had the house to do.'

Some might describe it as a *folie de grandeur* when you have a four-bedroom Georgian house to restore, but Fisher is the founder of Jamb, a Pimlico-based company selling antiques, lighting and reproduction chimneypieces, so is inclined to such eccentricities.

Perhaps his wife, Charlotte, has the upper hand in the house – now finished – where all is muted and pared down. She is banned from interfering in the garden, so her influence stops at the folding glass doors that connect the basement kitchen to a terrace.

Leading up to the main part of the garden is a Portland stone staircase, which began life on a grand country estate. This is the point where, as Charlotte puts it, Fisher morphs from a collector and dealer with a famously good eye and sense of taste into Liberace, the late American entertainer whose flamboyance knew no bounds. Terracotta pots line the steps like gentlemen of the chorus standing in salute, while a wave of sarcococca bushes underplanted with a lime green carpet of helxine rolls out along the top of its balustrades.

Until a few weeks ago, the garden was littered with architectural fragments, busts of Roman gods, urns and stone containers, which was more Caesar's Palace,

Las Vegas, than south London suburb. Jamb is moving premises, and this, together with two small children who are not particularly suited to a house and garden stuffed with antiques, encouraged Fisher to have a clear-out.

About five hundred lots, including the contents of several shipping containers full of furniture and objects, are to be sold at Christie's next month. Garden objects range from the humble, such as twenty terracotta pots (estimated at £300–£500 for the lot), to the grand – an eighteenth-century statue of the goddess Juno has a guide price of £10,000–£15,000.

The chaps from Christie's have had their pick, but it is hardly as if Fisher's garden has been left bare. He has discovered that plants are a rather cheaper way of adding architectural structure and grandeur. He proudly shows off a holly, clipped into a narrow cone, which he was amazed to find cost only £99. This might seem rather a lot to most gardeners, but it is all relative when you usually deal

Will 'Liberace' Fisher and his wife, Charlotte, on the weathered steps leading from the garden to the basement.

in objects that cost thousands. Giant box balls fill the terracotta pots, a viburnum is clipped into a mushroom shape and shapely ferns line the bottom of the walls in shady areas.

Two potted lemon trees dominate the centre of the garden. They were given to Fisher by Lord Howard of Rising, a friend and client, who said his wife would divorce him if he kept them, because of their bulk and neediness. Fisher fears they may provoke the same reaction from Charlotte, as they are too heavy to move. He is protecting them from the frost with 8-foot-high plastic boxes, which do not add to the aesthetic appeal of the wintry garden.

A couple of olive trees planted in a far corner may contribute yet another Italianate touch, but are incongruously rustic at this time of year. Once the herbaceous border comes back to life in the summer, however, providing a burgeoning mass of colour and informality, they will sit more comfortably. They're not quite in the Gertrude Jekyll, English country garden style that Fisher is hoping to achieve with the border, but, like his eclectic taste in antiques (anyone for a Victorian stuffed chihuahua? – there are two in the sale), they are all part of the exuberant spirit of the place. Fisher's approach is 'bung it in and see if it grows – what I lack in plant knowledge, I've made up for in enthusiasm.'

For the time being, thanks to winter and the sale, the Liberace of Camberwell has removed his toupee and is resting between acts. But it won't be long before the house and garden fill up again. 'You don't ever get it out of your system,' he says. 'The pleasure is in the buying.'

15 January 2012

Left The pond, home to three large koi carp, is hidden behind a tall brick wall at the far end of the garden. The blue doors lead not to the church but to the pond's pump system.

Right Because it incorporates the view of the church, and is full of layers of trees, bushes and pots, the garden appears larger than it actually is.

The Christie's auction raised £3.9 million, one of the stuffed chihuahuas fetching £20,000 – forty times its estimate. Fisher and family continue to live in Camberwell.

ANA TZAREV

Cap Ferrat, France

Ana Tzarev doesn't wait for the butler to do the honours, but comes down the steps of La Fleur du Cap, her home on Cap Ferrat, to greet me. It's a privilege in more ways than one – this is the first time the Croatian artist has allowed a publication to see what lies behind the front door of one of the most iconic houses on the French Riviera. Somerset Maugham, who had a house on the Cap, once described the Provençal peninsula as 'the escape hatch from Monaco for those burdened with taste'. Charlie Chaplin used to take the house (built in 1880 and called Lo Scoglietto until Tzarev changed the name) for the summer, and it was bought by David Niven, that most elegantly suave of English actors and raconteurs, in the early 1960s. The house briefly appears in *Trail of the Pink Panther*, one of his last films.

Niven died in 1983, and many of the homes in the area where he mixed with the beau monde have been bought in recent years by Russian oligarchs and billionaire

Ana Tzarev, hard at work in the garden, where she paints every day.

businessmen. La Fleur du Cap, however, has not faded – the dusky pink house is visible for half a mile along Promenade Maurice Rouvier, the coastal path that runs down the eastern side of the peninsula from Beaulieu-sur-Mer.

The butler pours us a glass of champagne in the high-ceilinged, gilded drawing room, where the walls are hung with Tzarev's paintings. Having taken up a brush at the age of fifty-six, two decades ago, she now paints with impressive energy, producing thousands of pieces. These are displayed in her eponymous gallery in Manhattan and in shows around the world; this month, they can be seen in London, at the Saatchi Gallery. 'I work all day,' she says. 'I don't communicate with anybody. I don't accept any invitations to parties. I don't go out at all.'

The pictures – of subjects as wide-ranging as Russian folk tales and kabuki theatre – have eye-watering price tags, with oil paintings starting at $100,000. As to who buys, and in what quantity, the director of the Ana Tzarev Gallery, Simone DiLaura, says clients are European, Asian and American, but is tight-lipped about names and numbers: 'We don't disclose information on sales.' The works have yet to come up for auction on the open market.

Tzarev's artistic ambitions have been helped by seemingly inexhaustible reservoirs of financial back-up and cheerful self-belief: 'I feel spiritual. That gives me licence to be courageous and do what my spirit tells me.'

Yet life was not always so privileged. Born Marija Guina in Trogir in 1937 (Ana Tzarev is her mother's maiden name), she grew up under the deprivations

La Fleur du Cap in all its pink glory.

of Marshal Tito's communist regime. At the age of nineteen, she caught the eye of a New Zealander, Robert Chandler, who was touring Europe with a friend; some weeks later, he returned to Yugoslavia to take her to his native country as his bride. They have been married for fifty-six years, and Robert, now eighty-nine, stays at his desk as his wife talks about her work and the story of finding the house. He maintains the benign air of a man who has heard his beloved's anecdotes many times before, polished to a sheen that would do Niven proud.

The couple have lived at La Fleur du Cap for only twelve years, but the property has long been in Tzarev's heart. Back in the late 1960s, she spotted a picture in a New Zealand magazine of Niven at the pink-painted property, and pinned it behind the sink so she could dream of it while she did the washing-up and tended to her three sons. Built into the coastal rock, it had Italianate arches and steps going down to a natural harbour. 'This is my house – I recognize it,' she would say, as she scrubbed the pans.

Thirty years later things were rather different, and doing the washing-up was a thing of the past. The couple had sold Chandler House, their chain of department stores in New Zealand, and moved to Monaco, along with two of their sons, Richard and Christopher.

Christopher rang his mother one day: 'I have a property to show you that you would be interested in.' She replied, as only a woman with access to a large fortune can do in an area with some of the highest property prices in the world: 'I'm not interested in anywhere where you can't see the sea. My soul is in the water.'

Christopher brought her to the house of her dreams, where she could indeed see the sea: it laps around most of the property under the pines that shade the rocks below. (The house is one of only fifty or so on the Cap with a coastal location.) They were met by Niven's widow, Hjordis. She showed them the fabulous views, painted by Winston Churchill, who used to visit on Sunday afternoons when staying nearby; the nineteenth-century rotunda, used as a set in the early days of film; and the study overlooking the sea, where Chaplin would write. Despite all this, Tzarev wasn't convinced. 'They wanted an absolute fortune,' she recalls. (It was advertised in *The Times* in 1996 for €12.5 million.) I said to Christopher that there was no way, not for that old wreck and ruin, and he said, "Well, it is your house. You wanted it."'

Three years later, the dutiful son took her back to the house, now even more run-down than before, but priced more realistically. (She won't say how much.) 'Christopher said to me, "You loved the place so much before. What if we do it up for you – will you consider it?"' What mother could resist? They needed three years to bring the now four-bedroom house and garden to their present immaculate condition, with new foundations, walls and windows, air conditioning and central heating. 'It took a lot of money and effort,' Tzarev says. 'I wanted it to function as a modern house but in a traditional sense.'

Yet it is the garden she loves most: 'I felt that it had been in my spirit for decades.' Tzarev doesn't bother with winter flowers – come October, she and Robert migrate to their home in Phuket, Thailand, until the following May. 'Everything I plant has to be in bloom when I am here,' she says. 'I am not interested in winter.'

Tzarev now also makes sculptures. This one, *Lovers*, has pride of place in the garden.

Accordingly, the pots and borders are filled with flowers – old-fashioned roses, oleander, bougainvillea, poppies, clematis and geraniums, largely in shades of pink and red. 'I wanted to bring in a natural flow of water, light and shade, the colour of the seasons in the flowers,' she says, although this is nature taken firmly in hand. The plants sit in a framework of a manicured lawn, dotted with palms, cypresses and olive trees, tweaked and tonsured to perfection. It's all a far cry from her first gardens in Trogir, planted in rusty old Red Cross milk-powder tins.

A gleaming white stone path leads down to the rose-covered rotunda. Beside this is a large air-conditioned studio, where Tzarev keeps a stack of canvases and paints. The garden is her inspiration, and many of the plants, including the huge hybrid hibiscuses that she grows in pots, will end up on canvas, depicted close up and larger than life, with bold colours and sweeping brushstrokes.

Tzarev has taken space at the Saatchi Gallery to show off her flower paintings. The exhibition also includes a 10-foot-high fibreglass sculpture of a poppy, painted in metallic red. 'I live and breathe flowers, and I thought, "Why not do the biggest flower in the world?"' She commissioned the work from a boatyard in Thailand and shipped it over in pieces to London. 'Everybody told me it was not possible.' The challenge was on, and she proved them wrong.

3 June 2012

Tzarev continues to paint every day, exhibits around the world and has added bronze sculptures, also on a grand scale, to her repertoire. She reports that she has made 'large improvements' to the garden 'with additions of botanic interest', and that the bougainvillea covering the house is photographed by hundreds of tourists as they pass.

JUDITH PILLSBURY

Provence

When you go into one of the many boutiques that cater to well-heeled visitors and second-homers in Bonnieux, a pretty hilltop village in the Luberon, the racks are hung in a symphony of beige. Taupe, ecru, biscuit, string – the muted tones are perfectly in accord with the pale limestone that dominates the area.

Nicole de Vésian, who lived at La Louve, on the lower slopes of the village, was a great lover of beige, and dressed in it all the time. While in Britain that might be considered a pasty choice, here in Provence, worn with a tan, it is a sign of refined good taste. The garden she created at La Louve, named after the last she-wolf to be caught in the region, creates the same impression – but in green.

Flowers are few and far between in the garden, which was created from scratch by de Vésian between 1986 and 1996, and is now owned by Judith Pillsbury, a retired American art dealer who has lived in France since 1965. It has irises and climbing roses, the odd hollyhock, a few clumps of achillea and incongruously dazzling gaillardias (a de Vésian favourite), but its main beauty lies in the trees, shrubs and subshrubs, clipped so that their shapes meld into the contours of the countryside beyond. 'The genius of this garden is how it reflects the landscape,' says Pillsbury, who also owns a house and garden in central Paris.

De Vésian, who was well known as a product designer for the luxury French brand Hermès, bought La Louve after she retired. The property, hanging on a steep hillside, was then owned by an elderly local man and the outdoor space was a mess. She created a four-bedroom house (it now has three bedrooms) and an adjoining orangery. Both have a simple quality, yet are highly sophisticated in their restrained use of materials.

Likewise the half-acre garden, which is arranged in steep terraces running down from the house. The plants are far from fancy, and grow happily and often wild in this arid region – box, *Viburnum tinus*, sage, myrtle, lavender and rosemary, for example. Yet the way they are arranged, with contrasting shades and textures, tightly clipped into soft mounds, has made the garden internationally famous, so much so that it has been classed as a *Jardin Remarquable* by the French government, one of only six in the region. If ever there were an example of 'less is more', La Louve, which is almost Japanese in its understatement, is it.

There are no lawns, as it would be hard to heave a mower up and down the levels, let alone keep grass verdant in the hot summer months. Instead, pebbles and gravel feature, along with pieces of stone chosen by de Vésian for their

Judith Pillsbury, on one of the terraces at La Louve.

innate beauty, in much the same way as she arranged the plants into tapestries of texture, light and shade. On the lowest level, which can be viewed from above, the layout is more formal than elsewhere, with a grid of lavender bushes that have alternative diagonal rows left unclipped to achieve different colours and textures, the purple haze of the flowering bushes contrasting with the silver tones of the clipped ones. Such a simple scheme is effective and eminently copyable.

Pillsbury admits that, as the lavender bushes last only seven or eight years before they get leggy and woody, spoiling the effect, she might have given up on this element if she didn't have extra help in the garden. 'One year, I planted it just with flax,' she says. 'That was beautiful and much easier to take care of.' The striking crosses of lavender and rosemary, which pay homage to the area's Cistercian architecture, also tend to get a bit woody: 'Nicole was a designer rather than a gardener.' In other words, the plants are servants to the overall picture.

One of the most remarkable things about La Louve is the fame it achieved in such a short time, bringing de Vésian a late career as a garden designer for clients inspired by what they saw there. Its creation coincided with a flowering of garden magazines and books, and it soon caught the editorial eye: all those architectural plants sitting so comfortably in the Provençal landscape looked fantastic in photos. These included the flat-topped cypresses, their tips removed initially as a practicality: they had been caught by frost and de Vésian didn't have the money for new trees. Later, they became something of a design signature.

La Louve's influence soon spread, and it is still popular with gardening groups, who are granted the occasional visit. 'There wasn't a Provençal style of gardening for this kind of climate – minus 10C in winter, 30C in summer – and on bad, stony land,' Pillsbury says. 'Until then, it had been much more an English cottage garden/Riviera style, in so far as one could try to do that – it was hard to succeed, as you needed tons of water. This seems a much more ecological approach.'

Sadly, osteoporosis caught up with de Vésian and climbing up and down the levels became too much, so she decided to sell. Pillsbury, who was recently divorced and looking for a new house, heard about La Louve from a mutual friend and arranged to go there for lunch. 'I arrived at 1 p.m. and she immediately took me out into the garden,' she recalls. 'I fell in love both with the garden and with her.'

Pillsbury bought the property for about £640,000 in 1996. De Vésian had already found another home at the top of the village, which needed some work. 'The idea was that she was going to share La Louve with me for about a year, as she was building her new house, though I think it would have been painful for both of us. Anyway, she had a heart attack and died two weeks after we signed the *promis de vente*.'

Pillsbury has made a few changes to the garden, such as installing a pool on the bottom terrace, on land that in de Vésian's day belonged to a neighbour, and adding a summer kitchen up at the top, where her predecessor had the orangery.

Looking down on the lavender bushes, alternate rows clipped and unclipped. The squared-off tops of the cypress became a de Vésian trademark design detail.

A mature tree on the top terrace had to go, as it was casting too much shade, and many of the shrubs have grown large in the thirty years or so since they were first planted. She has kept to the spirit of the place, though. 'I have loved it,' she says. 'I was definitely buying a work of art, and I felt I was given the chance to buy a small version of Sissinghurst – something perfect and gem-like that had been created by a woman.'

Now Pillsbury is leaving, love being as much a reason for selling as it was for buying. Four years ago, she married an Englishman, William Waterfield, and with him came another garden. He lives at Le Clos du Peyronnet, in Menton, on the Côte d'Azur (see page 22), so she is dividing her time between three houses at the moment. 'I didn't want to give up Paris, and it is expensive to run this. I couldn't very well ask William to give up what is a family garden – I had only been here for fifteen years. It seemed to be the right choice.'

12 August 2012

Left Stone, gravel and clipped evergreens are all that's needed on the terrace near the kitchen garden.
Above A path wide enough for a wheelbarrow curves down the steep hill.

La Louve was sold in 2014 to a couple from Normandy who open the garden on occasion. Pillsbury divides her time between Paris and Menton, where she largely leaves the gardening to her husband.

LORD CARRINGTON

Buckinghamshire

After lunch in the elegant dining room of his red-brick manor house in Bledlow, on the Buckinghamshire/Oxfordshire borders, where he has lived since 1945, Lord Carrington issues an invitation: 'Come and see the death of the swimming pool.'

'All tubes, this way!' he cries once outside, raising his stick in the air (he had a hip operation last year, though you would hardly know it), and the pack of dogs scuttling around at ankle level falls in behind. These include Sir Edward Heath and Dame Norma Minor, his portly miniature wire-haired dachshunds, but such is his air of benign authority that my own dachsy and the brace of terriers belonging to Robert Adams, the garden's designer, trot along too.

The 6th Baron Carrington, KG, GCMG, CH, MC, PC, DL, is well used to leadership. At ninety-four, he is the last surviving member of Winston Churchill's 1950s Conservative government, and he also served in six subsequent cabinets; he was foreign secretary under Margaret Thatcher from 1979 to 1982; secretary general of Nato from 1984 until 1988; and chairman of Christie's International auction house. Only the Duke of Edinburgh (two years younger) beats him in length of service on the Privy Council.

Yet, unlike many lesser men, he is not pompous or self-aggrandizing, giving full credit to Adams for the evolution of the garden over the past forty-five years, albeit with a tease or two. 'There is only one thing wrong with Robert, and it is a serious problem,' he says ominously, before a pregnant pause. 'He is much too modest – he doesn't push.' This brings a blush to the seventy-something designer's cheek. 'I've always said he is a promising lad.' So Carrington is going to do Adams's pushing for him, and we are off to see the new area of planting, which indeed signalled the death of the swimming pool and was completed in April. The pool was going to cost £25,000 to repair, which hardly seemed worth it for a few dips a year. In went the rubble from the dismantled pool, followed by 3 feet of topsoil. Where once the family dived in on a hot day, there is now a brick and paved terrace brimming with nepeta, artemisia and other lovers of hot, dry conditions.

A new wooden bench, in front of a curved wooden screen supporting 'Albertine' and 'Maid of Kent' roses, invites you to linger. 'There was a criticism from the daughters [Alexandra and Virginia] that there was no place to sit in this garden,' says Adams – 'Rubbish!' exclaims Carrington in the background – 'so we thought something more private and personal would work.'

'I'd better open up the pearly gates,' Carrington says, but he only means the glass doors of the former pool house, clad by Adams in a silvery cedar that matches

Lord Carrington and the designer Robert Adams, 'a promising lad' who has been working on the garden at Bledlow since 1968.

the trellis bearing a grapevine beside it. Inside, there's a display of black-and-white aeronautical photos of Sir Francis McClean, father of Iona, the late Lady Carrington: 'The second man to fly – a great pioneer. He started on balloons, then got interested in aeroplanes,' says his son-in-law. 'He was a lovely man.'

Near the pool house, and backed by the high yew hedge that separates the garden from the road outside, is a sculpture of a vulture, given to her husband by Lady Carrington, who died in 2009, aged eighty-nine – though, unfortunately, nobody can remember who it is by. It forms a focal point at the end of the red-brick path that connects this newest part of the garden to one created only three years ago in memory of Lady Carrington. Her presence is still very much felt by her husband of sixty-seven years, who constantly refers to her, painting with deep affection and respect a picture of she-who-must-be-obeyed.

At the far end of the path is a tulip tree, planted in the 1950s and a remnant of the rough area of trees, grass and bulbs that was there before. Lady Carrington was particularly keen on roses, and knowledgeable about them, so Adams has gone to town on these, creating a semicircle of climbing roses – mostly varieties from David Austin – arranged on ropes hung in swags between posts. They will spread to provide a wall of scent.

When put on the spot, Adams can't quite remember which varieties were chosen, other than that they were favourites of the family. One suspects that

Looking along the brick path towards the garden created in memory of
Lady Carrington, and a group of trees planted in the 1950s.

Lady Carrington, a keen plantswoman, would have been able to reel off their
Latin names. She obviously had strong opinions on roses, as they were the only
thing she disagreed with Adams about – though never seriously, he reassures.
'I'm all in favour of arguing about plants – about design, I have firmer views.'

As if that weren't enough, in the months between designing these recent
gardens, Adams squeezed in sorting out a raised bed beside a series of formal
brick-edged pools, located across the immaculately striped lawn in front of the
house. Full of bindweed, 'it was a herbaceous border that was out of control,'
Carrington says. 'So I said, in a Napoleonic way, "Get rid of it. Go away and get
the muse thinking."' The muse came up with a simpler scheme of Portuguese
laurels, Japanese quinces on the walls and herbaceous planting, including
lavender, heuchera and nepeta.

These creations are but the latest in a long collaboration between the
Carringtons and Adams. First brought in to sort out the mess left when a
thirteenth-century tithe barn burnt down outside the sitting-room window in
the 1960s, over the years Adams has transformed the six acres or so around the
house into an immaculate space, divided into 'rooms' of formal greenery, wide,
pinstriped lawns (Carrington has offered the gardeners a ride-on mower, but
they insist on doing it the hard way), herbaceous borders and, in a former cow
paddock, a sculpture garden with curving beds of mature trees and shrubs.

All this has emerged out of the scrappy farmyard and fields that the young couple inherited when they moved to Bledlow after the war, with only one or two beech trees and some elms (now long gone). 'We had such fun – think of the boredom of inheriting a garden,' Carrington says. While he plays down his part in its making, the many trees – 'I planted every single one you can see' – have provided a framework for the more ephemeral planting. And he can now enjoy them in their maturity.

In the 1990s, the formal garden had reached the gate beside a lane, and the Carringtons, then in their seventies, could quite reasonably have considered winding down a little in terms of digging and managing a garden. 'That's when my wife said, "That's enough."' But Carrington had other ideas, concerning the paddock across the lane. 'I said to Iona, "We will take in two and a half acres and have another garden." "No, you won't," she said. So we had a stand-off for about six months. Most unusually, I won.'

When he told her it was to be a sculpture garden, 'she replied, coldly: "You have no sculptures."' He sorted that out by ringing the professor of sculpture at the Royal College of Art and asking to meet some of his best students. 'Out of the car came some fairly odd-looking people who, when you got over their appearance, were absolutely delightful.'

He commissioned two of them – Paul Vanstone and Alistair Lambert – 'and that is how we started. It has been great fun.' Today there are a dozen works in the garden, each in its own space, hidden from the others, and including works by Peter Randall-Page and Michael Cooper.

Although the garden opens occasionally for groups, fetes and the National Gardens Scheme, it is essentially a private one. Across the road, though, in a steep gully, is the Lyde, a water garden created for the enjoyment of the village in the mid-1980s and open all year. Again designed by Adams, this is much more naturalistic than that surrounding the house.

As we walk back from the sculpture garden, as well as praising the team of three gardeners, headed by Mark Thompson, who have kept the place so beautifully, Adams fully appreciates how fortunate he has been to have had such a long and happy relationship with his employer. 'He has been a traditional patron. He is such a fantastic man – he has time for all of us. Every time you finish something, you think, "You lucky so-and-so", and he thinks of something else.'

Carrington hasn't heard this, but he says, not for the first time that day: 'We have got to think of something new to do, Robert.' And he will.

14 July 2013

They did find something new to do: revising the area to the south front, where the very first garden was created in 1968. The overgrown roses have been replaced with new shrub roses, with formal patterned planting in the foreground. 'The revision is the last work to the garden in terms of design,' says Adams, 'although I am pleased to report that the garden is being looked after as well as ever.'

SAM MCKNIGHT

London

Sam McKnight, one of the world's most admired hair stylists, is an avid poster on Instagram. In among the dreamy scenes from Ibiza, where he spends the summer, and the selfies in a series of dreadful wigs, or backstage gurning with Cara Delevingne, pictures of dahlias and lupins, dewy petals and sunflowers in the dusk sneak into his feed.

At fifty-eight, McKnight has lately discovered the joy of gardening – a distinctly uncool activity in the eyes of most fashionistas – and is displaying the passion of a convert. Despite being deep in the spring/summer 2014 shows, he finds time to meet me at his home in Kilburn, north-west London, on a soggy afternoon, to show off the garden before the flowers go over. He flew in from Ibiza at 5 a.m. after a photoshoot with Kate Moss, is running an hour and a half late from a hair and make-up session for Paul Smith, and is en route to an appointment with Burberry – all in a normal day's work for a stylist who is still at the top of his game after more than thirty years in the business.

Unusually for such a fashion bigwig, there's not a flunky in sight. He is relaxed and cheery, hugely apologetic for being so tardy, and for having nothing to offer the photographer and me but a freshly dug carrot or a juicy tomato. The house is being renovated and won't be habitable until next year; until then, he is back in his old flat in nearby Maida Vale.

McKnight, who artfully mussed Daria Werbowy's mane for the cover of *Vogue*'s all-important September issue, is perhaps most famous as the man who gave Princess Diana a more informal coiffure in the last years of her life. But he has created several other iconic barnets: Agyness Deyn's bleach-blonde crop, Tilda Swinton channelling Bowie, Lady Gaga in a lilac wig. Moss, Madonna, Cate Blanchett, Sarah Jessica Parker and Kylie Minogue have had their tresses tamed by him – or not, as he often goes for the through-a-hedge-backwards natural look – and his styles regularly appear on the covers of the world's glossy magazines.

He bought the property and its 120 by 40 foot garden two years ago; he jokes that he bought the garden and it happened to come with a six-bedroom house. He fell in love with the outdoor space after seeing a photograph online, and plans to use some of the house as a studio.

As we chat, McKnight gathers tomatoes from raised planters in a south-facing spot at the end of the garden, snipping off stray shoots with the confidence of a man who has been sorting out untidy fringes for more than half his life. Despite the work, he makes regular visits to the garden to gather veg and keep an eye on the borders. (The tomatoes make an Instagram appearance later, arranged in a bowl ready for supper.)

The frenetic theatre of fashion weeks – London and Milan are under his belt by now; Paris is under way – with their frocks and front-row jostling, wigs and wedge cuts, seems a world away from this quiet corner of the capital. 'I have people around all the time, so I cherish my own time,' says McKnight, who lives alone. 'I can be here planting and deadheading, then think, "I need to put my glasses on, my eyes are going fuzzy" – and it is actually half-past nine at night. Time just goes.'

Although he has always loved flowers, and has visited gardens such as Great Dixter and Sissinghurst, this is the first he has owned himself. 'It's all new to me, I'm thoroughly enjoying it,' he says in an accent that has an undernote of his native Ayrshire, topped with a London twang and a hint of a mid-Atlantic drawl.

When he moved in, like many a city garden, it resembled a football pitch – mostly given to lawn, with narrow borders clinging to the fences round the edges. There were some established trees, including a fine pear and an apple on its last legs. The apple will stay, as it now supports a climbing rose and a clematis.

Sam McKnight, in the garden as it is in 2017. Like hair-styling, making a garden is 'all about shape, form, colour and texture'.

The high leylandii hedge, on the other hand, which screens next door's shed, will go once McKnight has worked out what to replace it with.

At the moment it makes a theatrical backdrop for the pots clustered in front of it while the patio is being relaid. Climbers creeping in from the neighbouring gardens are more welcome, and he has planted a clematis and a passion fruit, which are careering along a fence. A Virginia creeper covering a shed at the far end of the garden is standing by for its fiery autumn show.

New borders extend out into the lawn, dividing up the space, and McKnight has great plans for more once he has got his house back from the builders. There will be a glass wall on the back of the house, facing west, leading to the patio with an area for him to do his daily yoga, and spots for roses, veg and more.

Has his work changed since he took up the secateurs? When he's got a moment, he's going to compare his styling over the past two years with what he has been doing in the garden: 'It is all about shape, form, colour and texture.'

So far, in the garden, there's no topiary clipped into outlandish shapes. The borders are brimming and slightly unruly – at this time of year with the rich colours of rudbeckias, echinaceas, sunflowers and Japanese anemones. He admits they are not all his own work (he hasn't the time, so he has help with maintenance), but he's definitely got the bug. 'I'm learning about flowers as I go along. I've been loving taking pictures of them, getting really close to them and learning their names. It has been good for my mind – a memory exercise. For example, I take echinacea for colds, but I had no idea it was a beautiful flower. I first saw it growing next to sunflowers in a garden in Ibiza.'

Once the borders have become more established, there will have to be some editing, as McKnight admits to over-planting – a common mistake for new gardeners keen to see rapid results. He is learning to be patient and to plan ahead, though he won't be putting in any tulips this year (he favours the blowsy peony ones), as he won't be back in the house until May.

I can see I'm not going to get any catty gossip about his clients' bald patches, or difficult designers and badly behaved models. Despite his stellar status, McKnight remains one of the most down-to-earth and friendly people in an industry that has more than its share of giant egos and back-stabbers, and he is touchingly appreciative of all the opportunities his work has brought him.

He's not that keen on divas (though he probably has greater tolerance than most). 'I like being around nice, friendly people. I don't thrive on drama. I like people who are real.' That included Diana: 'She was just fantastic – we got on like a house on fire.'

Fashion and gardening seem worlds apart – the former disinclined towards mud and muck, and changing constantly; the latter in for the long haul, and working the Worzel Gummidge vibe, clothing-wise, season after season. Yet, having attended the Chelsea Flower Show with Davina McCall, and later the Hampton Court Flower Show (the floral equivalents of the catwalk), McKnight has found many similarities. 'It is not the instant gratification that fashion is, but there are a lot of parallels. People are so passionate about what they do. It is a visual thing, too – there is a lot of styling involved.'

With the help of the designer Jo Thompson, McKnight has extended the beds into the lawn, to maximize the area devoted to plants.

After so many years being always on the move, he has no intention of leaving fashion behind and devoting his time to his dahlias. His new love has been good for him, though. 'It has been nice for me to adopt a bit of a slower pace. I have spent years rushing around all over the place, working with huge egos. It has been fantastic, amazing. But it's equally wonderful to immerse myself in gardening and a bit of cooking.'

Next stop, he'd like a house not too far from the sea, in Dorset or Wiltshire – with some land. The seeds of contentment have been sown.

29 September 2013

Roses, inula, cardoons and monarda are among the jostle of plants in the new beds.

Four years on, McKnight is still overpacking his garden and this shows no sign of abating. When I revisit on a hot June morning, there are pots of gaura and geraniums bought on a photo shoot at Great Dixter the week before, waiting on the patio to be planted. The garden has changed dramatically, thanks in part to the contribution and friendship of Jo Thompson, a Chelsea gold-medal gardener whom McKnight met through the television presenter Davina McCall. Gone is the wide expanse of lawn – there is still grass but the borders take priority, curving round the grass to allow for maximum planting. The old apple tree at the centre has gone too – to be replaced by a beautifully shaped quince, which provides a focal point from the house.

McKnight is still thoroughly enjoying the place, and any earlier plans to move have foundered. 'It has been an amazing journey.' Now that the borders are considerably wider, there are more layers and greater depth to the planting, with inula, phlomis, valerian and day lilies providing the pops of midsummer colour; dahlias still feature heavily towards the latter part of the year. And there are roses everywhere, although in many cases he is rather at a loss over which varieties they are. Some maintenance workers moved them in their pots when the extension was being built and lost the labels. So, not only does he not know their names, he doesn't which of his friends they came from. If you recognize yours from his Instagram posts, do let him know, and he can thank you properly.

WILLIAM CHRISTIE
Pays de la Loire

It is quite something to have a garden listed as a *Monument Historique* in France – even more so when the garden is only thirty years old, and its creator is not even a native Frenchman. Although the harpsichordist and conductor William Christie has lived and worked in France since 1971, becoming one of the world's leading champions of baroque music, he hails from America. This is a country that was in its colonial infancy when the farmhouse at Le Bâtiment, deep in the Vendée countryside, was built in the early seventeenth century.

However, Christie has been showered with accolades by his adopted country, including membership of the *Légion d'Honneur,* for his commitment to reviving the popularity of the French composers Charpentier, Lully and Rameau, as well as other European music of the seventeenth and eighteenth centuries. His renowned *Les Arts Florissants* ensemble, which he formed in 1979, performs pieces from that period worldwide.

It is perhaps no surprise, then, to discover that Christie's love of the baroque extends further than the musical score. His home is on the outskirts of Thiré, a village about an hour's drive south of Nantes. Here he sings a song of praise to the formality of the period, both in the contemporary furnishings and wall hangings in the seven-bedroom house, and in the gardens, which cover five acres of formal spaces, with a further thirty or so acres of less 'gardened' land.

The formal part is divided up – a Dutch-influenced parterre in front of the house, an Italianate rose garden, a 'theatre' of yew clipped into swooping Chinese pagoda shapes, and a potager. A grand view over a *miroir d'eau* lake to a folly is backed by artfully landscaped woodlands on a distant hillside. Christie describes it as 'ordered' rather than formal, based on lines and vistas, motifs and crisp outlines, adagios and allegros of quiet green spaces enclosed by severely clipped hedges and topiary, followed by borders of intense colour.

Educated at Harvard and Yale, the tall, elegant Christie is amused that his creation has been described as 'breaking all the rules'.

'It infuriates some of the French historians, but this is an artist's house and an artist's garden. It's whimsical, poetic licence – every fantasy I've had since I was twelve years old,' he says, as we drink coffee in the tile-floored kitchen after a lunch of grilled sole, apple tart and vegetables from the garden, which he has cooked himself. If he wants to put a chinoiserie bridge next to the stream lined with pollarded willows, or topiary doves around the *pigeonnier* – which houses three hundred doves – he'll do it, although when it comes to structural plants he tries to stick to those that are at home in the area – yew, box, ash,

oak and hornbeam. It's not the place for exotic species trees introduced in later centuries, which would be at odds with the spirit of the place.

As with his music, he brings a twenty-first-century sensibility to the garden. 'It is my interpretation of a particular period in European history that I am fond of. There are citations, there are inspirations, there are winks, but it is eclectic as well. I am happy I am living now, in that I can go through the historical stuff – Italian mannerism and French seventeenth-century gardens – but I can also have a good wink at American and English Arts and Crafts gardens. I love Beatrix Farrand more than any of the English garden architects.'

Since its inception, his ensemble has gathered and practised at the house, so music has long filled its fifteen rooms. For the past two years, the garden, too, has been the *mise en scène* for a music festival, held over the last weekend of August and attracting seven thousand visitors this year. Parking at a nearby campsite, music fans cross over the stream to the 'wilderness areas', where they can picnic among the willows and white poplars at its perimeters before watching a performance on a floating stage in the lake, in the rose-filled cloister to the side of the house or in the Chinese yew 'theatre'.

The garden is also open for about forty days a year. 'If I had the option of opening it more, I would do so,' says Christie, who is often on the road. 'I'm very Bolshevik about it – people who can afford to should share. I have more than enough minutes when I can be by myself.' He's now thinking of a spring festival, with concerts in the village church and trips to the garden to admire the thousands of bulbs, including early snowdrops in the Italian garden, camassias and narcissi down by the stream, and 'Kingsblood' tulips in the orchard.

While the coast of the Vendée, an hour or so south-west, is a popular tourist destination, Christie's home is firmly in *la France profonde*, a gentle countryside of unremarkable villages and small towns, farms and fields that is far from chic. 'The area is still unknown, which is marvellous,' he says.

He came across the locality in the 1970s, when performing nearby, and fell in love with it, first renting a property, then buying a house, which he decided was too big. He wanted something he could restore, with no established garden at all, as he had a strong sense of what he would create himself.

Christie found what he was looking for in Thiré: a beautiful old house that had been tenanted for generations by impoverished farmers and was now unoccupied. 'I saw this most incredible facade, with tiny windows. I found the house, and what was around it was rotting old farm buildings, with two rusting automobile carcasses on the front lawn and an enormous oil drum for burning rubbish. That is exactly what I wanted.'

He is certainly a man of vision and determination. He had in his mind's eye what he wanted from the garden and the wider landscape, and it has taken him thirty patient years to sew it all together, buying parcels of land – fourteen in

It took Christie years to buy the land to create this vista, looking down from the house over the lake to the folly in the distance.

William Christie, in the cloister garden next to the house.

all – as they came up for sale. Nowadays, 'I pretty much have what I was able to see then, with some modifications. I wanted to have topiary. I wanted to have an Italian-style garden, the garden sloping down to the river. I wanted an immense hornbeam wall around the part of the garden near the house.'

He still has plans – a belvedere in the Italian garden to look down on the formal terrace and the lake, a new set of steps here and there. Yet he admits: 'I am thinking now about how I can retract. I have cut out an awful lot of work for myself, and I can't really see anything more being developed in terms of needing lots of intensive labour.' He has two full-time gardeners and seasonal extra help, as well as his own labour, but there are a lot of hedges to keep in perfectly crisp outline.

Despite the occasional outburst of riotous colour and herbaceous abundance, this garden is firmly under the conductor's baton, and a crisp rhythm prevails. One wonders what sort of garden Christie would have created if he had been a lover of, say, late romantic music, or Philip Glass. 'Would I have done a different garden? I can't answer that. When I think about this garden, I think of the music I love.'

10 November 2013

The first spring festival, which focuses on sacred music, was held in April 2017. William Christie has also introduced a new element at Thiré to encourage young garden designers: a competition to create a temporary garden in which performers will play as part of the August festival.

JIM CARTER
& IMELDA STAUNTON

London

O n the table in Jim Carter and Imelda Staunton's kitchen in north-west London is a circlet of orchids and faded mauve roses, lifted (with permission) from the set of Downton Abbey, which is filming this summer. The fifth series of the hugely popular television drama is up to 1924 now, and Carter's beetle-browed butler, Carson, is still in charge of the servants' hall. 'We have slowed down the gallop through time – otherwise it would be Carson trying to work out how to use a computer,' Carter says in those familiar deep Yorkshire tones, which sound like a weary bear gargling gravel.

We admire the arrangement, not least for using real flowers rather than fake ones; with average viewing figures of 11.8 million in Britain, and sales to 220 territories, the set dressers can afford such indulgences. The mauve roses were favourites of Staunton's beloved late mother, whose ashes lie under an ornamental cherry tree outside, although Carter isn't quite sure about the composition of the arrangement. 'It is a bit more structured than I would do,' he says as he brings a cafetiere of coffee to the table – sadly, not on a silver tray with a lacy doily.

What? Carson arranges flowers? One can imagine that Carter's alter ego, a stickler for tradition, would greet such a feminine task with about as much enthusiasm as if he had been asked to give Lady Edith's smalls a quick run-through. Carter, however, is keen. It all started when the couple decided to tackle the south-facing terraces at the side of the Edwardian house where they have lived for twenty-one years (they have been married since 1983). 'We did have vegetables here, but we were rubbish at it,' admits Staunton, who is taking the morning off before returning to the West End: she has won rave reviews for her role in *Good People*, by the American playwright David Lindsay-Abaire.

Staunton has a lead role as a pixie – well, she is five feet tall – alongside Angelina Jolie in *Maleficent*, Disney's latest offering, and has won several awards, including a Bafta for Mike Leigh's *Vera Drake*. She was awarded an OBE in 2006 for services to drama, but there's not a hint of luvviedom from her or Carter. They are down to earth and rather a hoot. Today, though, she is playing the under-gardener to Carter (or 'barky assistant', as she prefers).

With the veg gone, 'it was a shame to waste the sun on the warm wall, so we decided to do all cut flowers,' says Staunton. Carter went on a growing course with Sarah Raven: 'That was great, just to give me the confidence to have a go. Then, having done that, I thought, "What do you do with the bloody things?" so I went on a flower-arranging course, which was fantastic.' How did he find time in his packed schedule? 'It was just for the day, not a three-week course – it was full of simple ideas.'

Jim Carter and his 'barky assistant', Imelda Staunton, in their front garden.

The top terrace is now planted with dahlias, which overwinter in the shed, as well as annuals such as zinnias, cosmos and cornflowers. 'We go for bright,' says Carter. The lower terrace, meanwhile, houses tulips grown in pots last year and lifted after flowering. They, too, will be used for arranging should they come up again next spring.

The side return of a house is an area often rather neglected, but Carter and Staunton garden their plot intensely and little goes to waste. Indeed, it is rather charming to see how packed their front garden is – instead of the usual neglected patch with a few shrubs to catch wind-blown crisp packets, it is a generous feast for the eyes of passers-by. As for the colour scheme of bright oranges, purples and pinks, Carter concedes that it's 'bold'. 'We go for the Christopher Lloyd palette, rather than tasteful peachy creams.' There's a certain unruliness to it, too, which gives it the air of a country cottage garden. You can hardly discern the paths that run through it, so dense is the planting of perennials, bulbs and shrubs.

Molly, the family terrier, follows us to the back of the house, where there's a long lawn and a border packed with a sweet disorder of perennials, climbers and roses running down one side. A black-painted pavilion is tucked in by a pear tree, with a pond in front of it. Beyond, the garden slopes away past two large robinia trees, one of which recently died and will have to go.

Although it is a normal-sized suburban garden, the fact that it is on a hillside somehow makes it seem larger; it also means it is barely overlooked. In a garden above are a huge copper cherry and a magnolia; in another garden an old pear tree adds a sense of maturity to their own. 'We were saying the other day how lucky we are to have the backdrop of everyone's trees,' says Staunton.

Beyond the pavilion is a steep downward slope, newly furnished with ferns and woodland plants to replace the 'secret' play area once used by their daughter, Bessie; she's now twenty and studying at the Guildhall School of Music and Drama. In a corner at the bottom is a gate in the fence, leading to Hampstead Cricket Club's playing field. Its wide expanse of greenery can be glimpsed through the trees from the house, creating yet more sense of living in the countryside. This portal to the cricketing world is especially convenient for Carter, who is chairman there and spends much of his summer, when not filming, involved in such weighty matters as sorting out the tea rota and paying the umpires.

You'd think that such successful actors might have a house or two elsewhere, but their lives are so busy they hardly have time to enjoy this one. Being cast as a senior servant has its drawbacks; as Carter says, when they are filming *Downton*, 'Every time I'm upstairs, the kitchen staff have got a week off. Every time I'm downstairs, the posh people have got a week off.' Besides, as Staunton points out: 'We feel we *have* a house in the country, five stops from Bond Street.'

Then there's their garden, which they have largely created themselves over the past twenty years, as what was there when they bought the house was in a state of neglect. Time spent in it together is especially precious. 'Our favourite day is both of us pottering around,' says Carter. 'There are seats galore, because we sit down all the time and look at it. We knew nothing about gardening when we came. It was trial and error. We got bolder and bolder, and learnt to get rid of things that weren't working. I officially acknowledged middle age when Imelda bought me a greenhouse and I was happy.'

The couple's taste for horticulture has also nicely overlapped with their charity work. They recently became patrons of Greenfingers, which provides gardens for children's hospices – forty-one so far. As Staunton says: 'That's what fame is useful for – to do good stuff.' Carter agrees. 'It's brilliant. Whenever you think of a children's hospice, you think of the child with a life-limiting condition. Then, of course, there are the parents and the siblings.' The idea of the gardens is to give the family an enchanting place to go, with exciting things for the children to play on and let off steam.

So what about *Downton*? How many more formal dinners will Carson be presiding over? 'Nothing's concrete,' says Carter. 'It can't go on forever, or else we'll all be a hundred – in real life, too.' Meanwhile there is the garden to tend. 'Of course it is never done, is it? I would hate a garden that is formal and "done". We are not assiduous with the maintenance at all. Like our lifestyle has no pattern to it, our gardening doesn't, really.'

He confesses that, although they spend as much time as they can outside, it isn't all their own work; once a fortnight, someone comes in to weed and cut the grass. 'I can't bear drudgery of any kind. I do what is enjoyable. Blokes are meant to like mowing lawns. I can't stand it. Booooring.' I'm not sure Mr Carson would approve of such an attitude.

8 June 2014

The generous backdrop of mature trees creates a feeling of seclusion in the back garden.

Imelda Staunton was nominated for an Olivier Award for Good People *and went on to win* *Best Actress in a Musical the next year for her performance in* Gypsy. Downton Abbey *ran for another series, then we said goodbye, after a Christmas special in 2016. Carter and Staunton have made a few changes to a part of the garden – Staunton reports she was up at 5.15 a.m. on the longest day of 2017, watering some young hornbeams – and they have no intention of moving. The garden 'gives us constant joy.'*

CAROL BRUCE

Kent

Carol Bruce is married to a successful property financier, so you might expect to find her driving a Range Rover through the Kent countryside and spending £100,000 on commissioning a smart garden designer to create a picture-perfect paradise, all without her having to get a nail dirty or a hair out of place.

Not so: Bruce drives the cheapest car she can find that will carry her dogs and bags of compost, and warns me that she will probably have twigs in her hair when we meet. She may indeed have spent £100,000 on her garden at Old Bladbean Stud, near Canterbury, but that has been over the course of ten years, and it is all her own work. For Bruce's idea of heaven is digging holes, and hiring someone else to do what she loves would be anathema.

Carol Bruce, at work in the pastels garden.

In fact, as the garden is open several times a year for charity events, she considers it to be her life's work. She has conjured up a veritable Sissinghurst of romance, spread over three and a half acres, by herself – give or take a brick wall or stone path – with her husband, Maitland, giving her a hand when he has time. 'If you want to live in a rainbow, you have to build one,' she says. (She is inclined to discuss the garden in such poetic terms.) 'I don't think you can pay someone to take that journey for you.'

Getting to the garden does indeed feel like a trip to the end of the rainbow. The single-lane tracks in the Kent Downs are so little used that they have grass growing down the middle. And when you get there, parking is in a rather scruffy farmyard. But once you pass through the wrought-iron gates in a high red-brick wall, you enter an enclosed world of abundant growth, with plants spilling over paths and jostling for space.

Bruce's 36-page guidebook, in which she cites Greek mythology, music, poetry and fairy tales as influences, makes it clear that she has thought of every relationship between plants, from juxtapositions to how they affect a particular sightline. There's no chance that she will have filled a random space with a nice perennial she picked up at a village fete; this is a garden where the overall mood takes precedence over the sum of its parts.

It would be easy to assume that Bruce had done a course at one of the upmarket garden design schools geared towards ladies who lunch, but this is not the case; she has learnt on the job since she started gardening sixteen years ago at her former home in Ashford. 'I took to it like a duck to water,' she recalls. Nor does she devour glossy magazines and books about other designers to glean ideas – she looks blank when I mention a few names. No, she already has her own clear picture of what she wants.

'I naturally think visually,' she says. 'It is easy for me to come up with a mental landscape to create. It's then a question of working backwards to create the look I have seen in my head. I am making a collage out of the image of a place, using flowers.' Indeed, it can take her years, and many plants, often grown from seed and selected for the right characteristics, to get the exact tone, shape or size she has seen in her head.

The surrounding countryside is a great influence in terms of shapes, patterns and moods: the fall of shadows in woodland; the way plants die naturally. She likes to keep the stems and seed heads after flowering is over. 'It is about expressing an idealized moment in nature,' she says. 'This is the canvas; the plants are the paintbox.'

Bruce will even accommodate the local wildlife: it is an uncommonly generous gardener who incorporates an existing rabbit path into the design of a rose garden. If things fail – seedlings get nibbled, combinations don't gel, the colours don't work out – well, that's half the fun. As she writes in her guidebook, 'As with a particle accelerator, the bigger the smash, the more I can learn from the wreckage.'

The garden is divided into five areas, and you can see the painterly approach in the shimmering hues of each section: one with predominantly old-fashioned roses; a yellow garden, to confine this uncompromising colour in one space; pastels, where Bruce experiments with differently shaped plants in the same colours; a long grassy walk flanked by double borders that almost exactly mirror each other; and a huge vegetable patch, where she grows enough to last the couple for the year.

The colours are predominantly silvers, blues, whites and pinks, in romantic arrangements of towering delphiniums, ranks of irises and clouds of phlox. There's no concession here to the fashion for loud, clashing oranges, pinks and reds – the kind you would find in old-fashioned plants such as zinnias and dahlias, which are the horticultural equivalent of nursery food with a splodge of ketchup on top. Bruce admits to having 'no sensory filters' and is sensitive to noise in whatever form it takes (including children), so she finds such brightness loud and jarring. Dahlias, for example, are like 'sticking Post-it notes around the garden'.

Instead, everything is calm and in harmony, with garden tasks following the seasons by a strict timetable, starting on 1 January – when she rakes off the dead stems she cut down the autumn before and hand-weeds the plant crowns – then pruning roses from 1 March, through picking and preserving fruit and veg in late September to tidying up the hedges in December.

The steps she takes to create a glorious garden are as important to Bruce as the results themselves, whether it is raising generations of seeds until she gets the plant she wants, or experimenting with combinations and planting conditions. As she writes: 'When an idea is pulled down out of the clouds and on to the ground, it is crossing the border into another country. Magic wands, crystal balls and time machines are seized at customs, and from here on the terrain is defined by restrictions, binding constraints, trade-offs, unknowables and the laws of physics.' Er, quite.

It's hard work and, according to Bruce, 'takes a certain stoic mentality. It is not a dream, it is reality. People are seduced by the high points, but you really need to be someone who likes digging holes. It is the stuff you do before February that makes it happen.' She never mulches or fertilizes – she likes hoeing too much, and 'all's well so far.' Nor does she water, apart from vegetables and new plants. 'In this way, I hope to allow my garden to evolve with changes in the climate over the longer term.'

She admits that she never goes on holiday, and one wonders if she ever gets much further than the end of the lane. Being 'passionate' about your garden is a hackneyed phrase, used by people who are pretty darned keen on their plants and how they're put together, but for whom, really, it's not a life-and-death matter. Meeting Bruce, one gets the feeling that, were she to be separated from her creation, she might wither.

'I never imagined that it would be acceptable to spend all my days doing something I love fundamentally,' she says. 'It is my baby, my journey, my evidence on the planet that I exist. This is my honest truth. This is myself.' And that is worth more than any amount of money can buy.

21 September 2014

Bruce is still working on the garden, which is open for the National Gardens Scheme on a few days a year. Her husband has since departed for pastures new, but, on the plus side, it gives her more time both for gardening and for her new interest: stitching. She sells her delicate beadwork jewellery inspired by the garden and the surrounding countryside on Etsy (ReweavingtheRainbow). 'It is turning out to be very a garden-compatible and engaging venture in its own right.'

One of the mirror borders, by the sharp-edged lawn.

LADY MOUNTBATTEN

Kent

At the age of ninety, and nowadays not so quick on her feet, Patricia Knatchbull, the Countess Mountbatten of Burma, apologizes that her two-acre garden isn't up to much: she's down to one part-time gardener at her home near Ashford, Kent. Pots of colourful annuals crowd cheerfully around the entrance, but otherwise the garden is largely laid to lawn. There are, however, some impressive trees and, in a far border along a red-brick wall, 'Lord Louis' and 'Mountbatten' roses, named after her father, the last viceroy of India, from whom she inherited her title by special retainer.

Lady Mountbatten may have cut back on her charitable commitments, as well as her flower beds, but one of the positions she has kept is president of the local branch of the British Legion. She is a great supporter of their work: 'They really do look after anybody who has had service connections, whether you are nineteen or ninety. They are a very good, supportive organization.'

The Flanders poppy, which the Legion sells to raise money and awareness each year, is a poignant memorial of those who died in war, but it is transient, whether pinned on a lapel in November or planted in the garden for summer colour. So today the Legion is launching a campaign to get Britain's gardeners to plant a tree, shrub or bulbs as a lasting commemoration of those who fought in the First World War. The campaign is being led by Frances de Bosdari, director of Ashridge Nurseries, in Somerset, whose brother is married to Lady Mountbatten's daughter Amanda. Whether it is £3 for twenty-five 'Remembrance' crocuses or £200 for the 'Westonbirt' collection of native trees, at least 50 per cent of sales of more than a hundred varieties supplied by the nursery will go to the charity. 'It will be nice to encourage others to join the scheme,' Lady Mountbatten says. 'The more you can get involved, the bigger the donation to the Legion.'

Lady Mountbatten is a great-great-granddaughter of Queen Victoria, cousin of the Duke of Edinburgh and godmother to Prince Charles, so her life has been privileged. Nevertheless, she knows a thing or two about conflict. Her father was the Supreme Allied Commander South East Asia during the Second World War, and she served in the Wrens for three years. Her late husband, Lord Brabourne (John Brabourne, a film producer), landed in Normandy a few days after D-Day and fought his way to the German border, where he was wounded. His elder brother, Norton, had been shot by the Germans in 1943 after escaping from a prison train.

Lady Mountbatten admits having rather enjoyed her own wartime experiences. 'I reckon those of my generation who survived the war without terrible losses and

Lady Mountbatten, who was a great supporter of the British Legion and president of the local branch.

injuries were lucky, as it gave you quite a different outlook on life.' She signed up as a signal rating before reluctantly becoming an officer so she could follow her father to the Far East. 'We had people from all over the country sharing cabins, and I think it was a great education for people who had not been outside their own family and friends very much.'

It was in Ceylon (now Sri Lanka) that she met the man who was to be her husband of fifty years. He was ADC first to Field Marshal Slim and later to her father. 'He was living in the house, so we got to know each other extremely well. He said he knew from the first day I was someone he wanted to marry. It took ages until I said yes.'

But it was another conflict that brought Lady Mountbatten to the world's attention in 1979: the murder by the IRA of her father, her mother-in-law and her fourteen-year-old son Nicholas, as well as Paul Maxwell, an Irish boy, on a fishing trip on a family holiday at their house in Sligo. Lady Brabourne, as she was then, her husband, and Timothy, Nicholas's twin, were horrifically injured. Lady Mountbatten says of Timothy, now forty-nine, who recently wrote a book called *From a Clear Blue Sky: Surviving the Mountbatten Bomb*: 'He is a wonderful man. He has decided that instead of being half a person, he would be two people.' She, too, has chosen to continue life with no apparent bitterness.

Trees remain the dominant feature of the two-acre garden, even though fifty-three were lost in the great storm of 1987.

The couple raised seven children in their home on the Brabourne family estate, Mersham Hatch, where she has lived for sixty-two years. Her oldest son, Norton, inherited Broadlands, Lord Mountbatten's home, while her second son, Michael John, owns Mersham Hatch, which covers 2,700 acres.

Bockhanger Wood is a plantation of hornbeams on the estate that has been there for a thousand years. Trees were a special love of Lord Brabourne's, and he taught his wife to appreciate the beauty of their leafless form in winter. He established thousands on the estate, replanting a woodland every time one of their children was born and naming it after them.

In the family's garden, they planted a blue cedar and a wellingtonia in the 1950s, both of which are well on their way to full size. A small cedar, planted for 'some birthday or other', will take over from an ancient chestnut that is dying.

It is lucky that the trees are still there. On the night of 15 October 1987, Lady Mountbatten took the dogs out at 11 p.m. and noticed a hot wind, with red sand in the air. The couple went to bed and slept soundly, but on waking in the morning, they noticed that the drive was strewn with old pines. Then they looked out into the other side of the garden. 'There was a wonderful old oak, close to the house, which was absolutely flat. My husband and I both burst into tears, which was extraordinary, as men didn't cry in those days. We couldn't believe it. Our garden isn't very big [well, everything's relative] – but we lost fifty-three trees. Everyone went around in a daze for a week or so, saying, "What has happened to all the trees?" They felt they had lost a really important part of the environment.'

In the estate's parkland, too, the younger trees that had been planted were flattened, while the older ones, which had formed the shelter belt and had seen a storm or two in their time, remained standing, like old soldiers. Lady Mountbatten seems to see this as a metaphor for life. 'They have had to withstand the normal slings and arrows of outrageous fortune. A certain amount of problems in life is probably quite good for you, in a sense.'

28 September 2014

Lady Mountbatten died on 3 June 2017, the day after she had given me permission, via Amanda, who was with her, to use this article, as long as it remained as much about the British Legion as herself.

STUART ROSE

Suffolk

Fresh from a solo walking trip in the Swiss Alps, Stuart Rose is showing off his holiday snaps in the spotless kitchen of his three-bedroom farmhouse near Woodbridge, Suffolk. 'Just look at that – unbelievable!' he enthuses, as we admire picture after picture of wildflower meadows and close-ups of tiny Alpine plants.

On the way back, the businessman, best known for his six-year tenure at the helm of Marks & Spencer, bumped into Sir John Major, the former prime minister, at Zurich airport. What did they discuss? Their mutual late-found love of gardens. These two Tory grandees are both city bred. 'I've never had a garden before,' Rose says in a cheery, booming voice that would carry well across a packed boardroom. 'My mum and dad were urban animals – my father is still in the flat in London where he's lived for sixty years. I'm a pot-plant boy.'

Rose bought the eighteenth-century farmhouse – he calls it a cottage, but it's rather more substantial than that – for three reasons: 'I had never had a house in the country, I wanted a wine cellar and I wanted a bit of land.' Today, the pot-plant boy is more of a forty-acre man. As we stand on the stone terrace behind the house, admiring the view, all the land we can see belongs to him. Near the house are herbaceous borders and a formal area, with wildflower meadows beyond; a large grassy area around the corner would make a great cricket pitch (Major would like that).

Not that the sprucely dressed Rose gets his own hands dirty – he swears he would love to dig in, but just doesn't have the time. Instead, he gives full credit to Xa Tollemache – a distinguished Chelsea gold-medal-winning designer who lives at nearby Helmingham Hall and joins us. Pete Hammond, Andy Last and Jenny Heaffey, who work on the garden and land, also get a name check.

It was chance that led him to this rural corner of Suffolk. On a wine trip to Burgundy, he spotted a pretty girl in the party. (His girlfriend, Anna Hartropp, has heard this story many times before.) Despite his best efforts, however, his charms were not working. 'Then it dawned on me that I had been trying to chat up this bird all day long, and she was as gay as anything.'

Despite his failure they became friends, and when he saw the Suffolk house that she shared with her partner, he was impressed: 'I said, if you ever want to sell this house, I would like to buy it.' Two years later, the couple broke up and he got the call. 'It was completely serendipitous. I was married at the time, and we came to have a look at it. My wife didn't particularly like it, but I did, and that was that. So we bought it.'

That was in 2000. Fifteen years on, he's been through divorce and changes in his career: he left M&S in 2011, having risen through the ranks to become CEO from 2004 to 2010, and executive chairman from 2008 until shortly before his departure. 'I was tempted to sell the house four or five years ago. Anyway, I decided to keep it and get rid of everything else.' Not quite everything – Rose still has a London home and he is chairman of the online supermarket Ocado. He also sits on the boards of several international companies. In order to reconfigure the house, Rose shut it down for a couple of years: 'Two years ago, it was like the Somme. Everything was dug up.' That's where Tollemache comes in, again more through serendipity than planning. She and her husband, Lord Tollemache, were round for supper, and Rose was telling her about the enormous estimate he'd had from another garden design company. 'Xa said, "Well, I will do your garden" – and off we went.'

Rose didn't have Versailles-like schemes in mind, which made things easier. 'This is not a grand house, and I wanted to stay true to its context.' There was also none of the faffing around and indecision that designers often have to put up with from their clients. 'I am interested in colour, in clothing, in decor,' he says. 'I can happily sit on the floor with swatches – but I have never done a garden. I know what I like, but I can't do it.'

Xa Tollemache and Stuart Rose, on the bridge that connects the garden to the meadowy area beyond.

'Not too much froth': the formal planting near the house.

Tollemache decided to approach things visually. 'I had worked out what I would do, so I brought photographs of things. He would say, "I don't like that. Yes, I like that. I like these colours. That's the look I like." It was so easy, as I then had a palette to work on, though he didn't know what the plants were.'

'I still don't!' Rose exclaims.

One of the most important things they did was to knock down the walled garden that was close to the house. 'It was dark, and I have a bit of an obsession with light, so I wanted to open everything out,' he recalls. 'We also get big skies in Suffolk, so I wanted to bring the outside in.' This he has also achieved at the centre of the house, where it connects with the adjacent former barn: huge plate-glass windows stand on either side.

Outside, what was once a tatty yard is now the formal area, with two rectangular pools and a minimal planting of clipped box and yew. A path has been cut through the meadow beyond, leading to a crescent-shaped mound made by Tollemache and her digger. This is not a designer who minds getting grubby; she did most of the herbaceous planting herself. The gardeners were impressed – and her a Lady, too.

As we tour the garden and the land beyond, Rose leads the party at a cracking pace, like the Pied Piper with a plane to catch. Just when Tollemache is explaining the planting combination by the sunny terrace, including cardoons, roses, alliums, lilies and irises in shades of purple, dark red and pink ('not too much froth'), he will call us over to admire his new box for nesting bees, to drink in the glories of a particular rose or to brush by a bush – 'Ah, just smell that lavender!'

This part of the garden is protected by a section of the old wall that Rose decided to keep as a windshield, and to create some privacy – though the lane that runs alongside the property is hardly the M25. An old apple store is now a summerhouse: the orchard behind it has been greatly added to, and is underplanted with wild flowers.

Rose and Tollemache agreed that the garden should sit comfortably between the house and the countryside beyond, which is why the more formal borders are hard up against the house, low enough to be seen through and over, with the scheme becoming looser and wilder as you walk away.

Although much of the wider landscape on the property was already in place – they moved some trees out of the way to create the long vista – the garden itself is impressively mature for something that, in horticultural terms, is in its infancy. The new tennis court – surrounded by rugosa roses and lavender – and the walled kitchen garden provide pockets of more intense planting, but don't jar with the bigger picture. And at the far end, beyond a field that the local farmer cuts for silage, is Rose's 'mini Monet garden', a pond with an arched bridge across it. Tollemache takes no credit for this area.

Rose is a keen cook, so there's a well-stocked herb bed by the kitchen door, and chickens scrabble about in a pen in the kitchen garden. He later sends me a picture of one of them, roasted with herbs, garlic, red onion and carrots – 'It's all my own!'

Being away from the garden on a regular basis has brought him a new joy: on his return, he notices the seasons changing and buds appearing, and can enjoy the vegetables that have ripened in his absence. 'I can genuinely say that I can sit in a really dull board meeting some time on a Wednesday, thinking, "Why am I doing this?" Then I think, "On Friday, I'll be in the garden picking something – be it strawberries or Swiss chard." It must be a sign of age.'

Slowing down is not always such a bad thing, whatever your age. Rose has come to accept that, with nature, you need to have patience – 'which I haven't got a lot of' – and that the best results aren't always instant. 'I can see it now. That bit between the beginning and the end is interesting in itself, but you were always focused on the end. So you missed the middle bits, when actually the middle bits have got something exciting. It is a bit of a commentary on life.'

5 July 2015

Stuart Rose reports that he is still in Suffolk and that the garden has developed further since my visit.

HARRISON BIRTWISTLE

Wiltshire

Sir Harrison Birtwistle, Companion of Honour and one of today's most important composers, has been busy of late. It was his eightieth birthday in July last year, which prompted celebration of his music around the world, including the UK premiere of his work *Responses: Sweet Disorder and the Carefully Careless*, and programmes at the Barbican, the Southbank Centre and the Proms.

The pace hasn't let up since: his operatic 'scena' *The Cure* was premiered at the Aldeburgh Festival in June, and in July he was one of the featured musicians at the Viitasaari contemporary festival in Finland. He has just finished a string quartet and is working on an orchestral piece for Daniel Barenboim.

'I only ever write to commission,' he says, before adding with a naughty smile, 'but I write what I want.' To cap it all, he's managed to squeeze in some improvements in his garden in the quiet Wiltshire town of Mere.

When he is not travelling, Birtwistle makes the journey down the garden every day to work in the wooden studio, raised on stilts at its far end. 'I usually weed on my way up and arrive with a handful of black stuff,' he says as he finishes chopping onions to make a Provençal *pissaladière* for his supper in the eighteenth-century former silk mill where he has lived for the past sixteen years.

He seems bemused by the idea that he should be doing anything other than working; spending more time with his tomatoes, perhaps, or snoozing over an Agatha Christie novel in the afternoon. 'I just keep going. It is what I do. It gets funny when you haven't got anything to do. I don't know how to do nothing.'

He even finds time to tend to those tomatoes growing in his lean-to greenhouse. Although he has a gardener, David Henson, to help, he is very much hands-on, mulching, planting, pruning and tying in; and he proudly shows me the frames for the trained trees that he made himself.

We stand at the kitchen window, drinking Japanese tea and looking out at a big terracotta pot of gaura on the terrace. Birtwistle got the idea from a Palladian villa in Italy where huge pots of them were neatly spaced out in a line. Here there is only one, but the haze of white-pink flowers blends nicely with the elegant, pink-tinged form of evening primrose growing on top of the retaining wall behind them.

'I didn't plant those,' he says, referring to the evening primrose. 'I can't bear them usually, because they are a horrible yellow.' Actually, he is rather pleased by this particular apparition; it's just that Birtwistle is not one to go over the top with enthusiasm. (He suggests that a recently published book of conversations should have been called *Structural Mutterings*.)

Whether the wild-card seeds were blown in by the wind or turned up in the compost, he encourages such unexpected notes – along with self-seeders such as alchemilla and marjoram – in a garden that is predominantly formal. 'All the things that plant themselves, it is a gift, the random aspects of it.' There are plenty of repeated motifs, including rows of neatly spaced large pots of hostas and hydrangeas (that Italian influence again), and a long line of lavender along one edge of the raised central pond. The trees are largely trained into espaliers and cordons, or – with newly planted quinces – in an 'avenue'. A pergola runs down one side of the garden and there are stone terraces at either end.

As it is in Birtwistle's music, which is hailed for its roots in tradition and myth, but its refusal to fit into any category, so it is in the flower beds. Setting out a firm structure 'in order to destroy it' is at the root of his work. 'I deal in random things, which save me from the cliché of intuition.'

Harrison Birtwistle, on the steps to his elevated studio at the far end of the garden.

And in the garden. 'This thing of formalism, if I thought about it and I was pressed, it is very much related to what I do in music.' He makes precise concepts, then rearranges them. 'If they were pictures, they would look like something that had fractured. It is as if you can see the sense of something, but it has a random thing as well.'

It seems apt that, like his music – and his mutterings – the garden poses something of an intellectual challenge. It's a topsy-turvy world in which rules are broken. At first glance, the terrace by the house appears to have been dug out from the higher ground that stretches across the garden's width and down one side. But, beyond this high ground – on which he has a lawn, shrubby borders and the fruit trees – and hidden from the house by a stand of bamboos, there's a secret Italianate garden on the same level as the house, with the formal pond taking centre stage.

The bones of the garden were in place when Birtwistle and his wife, Sheila, bought the place, but the previous inhabitant had grown vegetables where the pond now stands. Birtwistle called in Lorraine Johnson to cast her expert eye and do the planting, and it was she who suggested the pond instead. It is filled with mirror carp: 'They have been here fifteen years – they are like little pigs. They scruff around on the bottom. I had turtles for a while, but they disappeared.'

The pergola runs along the shady far wall and is underplanted with ferns. At the end is a terracotta pagoda, designed by Birtwistle and made by his son Adam, an artist. It has turned out to be something of a wildlife hotel: 'I've had all sorts of things living in it – I've had nests in it, bees in it.' Moths, on the other hand (Birtwistle's *The Moth Requiem* was first performed in 2012, and was played at the Proms in 2013), prefer the fennel in another part of the garden.

The pond is raised to the same level as the high ground, and it appears that the paths around it and a far terrace have also been excavated from the soil. It is only when Birtwistle explains that the garden is on the site of an early-twentieth-century workshop, added to the back of the silk factory when Wilton Carpets took it over, that the layout begins to make sense. The walls that enclose the space are those of the workshop, and the whole thing has been created on top of the old building's concrete floor.

It has been a matter of addition of soil, not subtraction: rather than the terrace and paths being dug down from ground level, as first appears, the earth for the bank was brought in and dumped from two doors down, when a neighbour was excavating to make room for a swimming pool before Birtwistle moved in. 'It is eccentric,' he says. 'Sometimes you come across great lumps of clay, then cinders, as if somebody has been smelting.'

Somehow it seems appropriate that the garden of a composer whose work is known for its elusive and challenging qualities should be equally so. 'It is a

The long pond is raised to the same height as the bank near the house, which was created with soil from a neighbouring garden.

magic garden, really,' Birtwistle says. 'It goes through quite a lot of stages – from the house, you don't know there is any water in it.'

It was his friend Robin Yapp, a wine merchant based up the road, who suggested that Birtwistle might be interested in the house when he and Sheila returned from living in France, where they had spent several years. It wasn't just a random purchase, though: the couple had lived in the area at the beginning of their married life, when Birtwistle was teaching at nearby Cranborne Chase School, and two of their three sons were born there. Although he originally hails from Accrington, Lancashire, and still speaks in the flat cadences of his upbringing, 'it is like the return of the native – I never intended to come back.'

Sheila died in 2012, after a long illness, and it is only recently that Birtwistle has turned his attention back to the garden, putting in a new terrace beneath the studio this year. He has installed a table sheltered by a canopy fashioned from wires stretching between two of the iron roof pillars from the old workshop, which are painted a striking ochre to match the canes of the bamboos growing by the studio. Young vines are already scrambling up the wires.

There is an emphasis on strong outlines, whether it is in the formal layout or plants such as acanthus, agapanthus and cardoons, rather than a loose, romantic overflow of colourful flowers. 'It is difficult to know how it would be any different. It is all governed by the central water and the fundamental architecture.'

There is, however, plenty of room for edibles. Birtwistle is a keen chef, although he says, with a characteristic Eeyore shrug: 'I have no ambition about cooking, but people seem to like my cooking. I have no pretensions – I just cook.' He gathers apples, apricots, plums, quinces and pears from the garden, and gives me gives me a bag of plums to take home. The tomatoes are ripening in the greenhouse, and the cardoons and artichokes that he has just planted are growing like topsy in a border mulched with gunk gathered from the bottom of the pond.

There's also a decent herb garden. Birtwistle picks a sprig of thyme for me to sniff. 'It is a very particular one,' he says. 'It comes from Greece. It is what they use in black puddings in Lancashire, and it was always a secret. It smells like Bury black puddings.' With that secret revealed, we go inside to rescue the onions from the stove.

13 September 2015

Deep Time, *Birtwistle's collaboration with Daniel Barenboim, was premiered in Berlin 2017 and at the BBC Proms in London later in the year. He continues to garden: 'I love order but I can't quite create it.'*

Jilly Cooper ii

Gloucestershire

This article is a little off-piste, but it is here for those who – like Jilly Cooper (and me) – have shared their lives with beloved pets.

One of Jilly Cooper's favourite quotes is the answer made by her late husband, Leo, when asked what his wife wore in bed: 'Dogs.' Cooper is famous for her love of animals, which are accorded as much honour as the human characters in the sexily rumbustious tales from the shires that have made her novels beloved by generations of readers.

She's down to one companion at present – Bluebell, a seven-year-old black rescue greyhound – but the cats, dogs and occasional hamster in the family that have gone to the great basket in the sky are still very much with her. On every surface in her home are pictures of them – paintings in the hall, crowded photomontages in the kitchen, cushions with their faces printed on. There's a calendar, on which each month features the famous author clutching at least one greyhound, and a rather moving greyhound print by Judy Zatonski, where the dog's body is made up of the names of those that have departed.

However, it is in the grounds of Cooper's sprawling country house in Bisley, Gloucestershire, that the animals have their true tribute. In a woodland area on the edge of the garden, beyond the old tennis court and overlooking the field where the dogs once ran and the cats hunted, is her pet cemetery. At least twenty animals are buried here, each accorded its own gravestone and inscription, be it William, 'who conquered all our hearts', Feather, whose 'noble heart only failed because he gave so much of it away', or Mabel, 'now with the angels, where she belongs'.

A jug of flowers stands beside a temporary wooden cross and a large blanket of stones covers the latest, who died only a few weeks ago: Bobbie Tarrant, a yellow Labrador. Bobbie actually belonged to Cooper's daughter, Emily, but he spent much of his time here with his 'girlfriend' Bluebell, who accompanies us to the graveyard and lies lugubriously among the fallen leaves as we talk of pets past. There's Hero, and Barbara, Mabel's fellow mongrel, who came with Cooper and Leo when they moved from Putney thirty-two years ago. And the Pub Cat: 'Leo said, "We are not having any more animals." Then the first time he came off the train from London, it was with a juddering cat basket,' laughs Cooper. Socks and Feral, along with Bessie the black Lab, are here too. 'I spend a lot of time at the graves, sitting talking to them, especially in the summer,' Cooper says.

And it would appear she is not alone in wanting to commemorate her animals – *The Times* has even set up an Animal Life section of its register pages. Entries among the pictures of dear departed pets include an In Memoriam to Tuvoc, the Russian blue badger rat, 'a father of three with numerous grandchildren', who died earlier this year aged thirty-nine months.

RIP Tuvoc on this, the eve of All Souls' Day – although the Catholic Answers website, which I consulted as to whether animals actually have souls, states that yes, they do, but only until death – 'There is no doggie heaven,' it states, rather harshly.

The ancient Egyptians, who mummified their cats, would query this, believing them to be deities. However, in more recent times, it is memories of our animals' companionship we want to acknowledge, whether they are up there in the clouds or not. There are a few public pet cemeteries scattered throughout the UK, though ground maintenance fees make them an expensive option. Cremation is a more popular choice, although, if you want to be sure you are being given back the right remains, it is best to go to one of the thirty-seven members of the Association of Private Pet Cemeteries and Crematoria.

You may, like Cooper, want to have your animal closer to home. According to PFMA, the pet food manufacturers' association, nearly half the households in the country own a pet of some sort, be it a rat, goldfish or dog. That is a lot of animals that at some point will become ex-pets. Some will end up flushed down the loo (goldfish); most will be incinerated by the vet. You can even get them taxidermied, but it is perfectly legal to bury them in your garden.

You'd be in a fine tradition: many country estates have an area set aside for their pet cemetery, including Sandringham in Norfolk, where a quiet corner is reserved for the Queen's corgis. Some special animals are even accorded their own place of honour. For example, the Duke of Wellington's charger Copenhagen, who carried him throughout the Battle of Waterloo and died in 1836 aged twenty-eight, is buried at Wellington's home, Stratfield Saye, in Hampshire, beneath a large turkey oak, planted as an acorn in 1843. And at the centre of Rousham, in Oxfordshire, one of the jewels of early-eighteenth-century English landscaping, there is a grotto with a marble plaque in honour of Ringwood, 'an otter hound of extraordinary sagacity'.

While not all of us have the space to spare for a 15-hand horse or generations of Welsh ankle-biters, most people should be able to find a quiet corner in their garden, especially if an animal has been cremated. There are a few things to consider if you are burying the body, though: first that you are the legal owner of the land – you don't want to give the landlords a fright when they try to plant their potatoes in the spot after you've gone.

The body should not be 'hazardous waste' (in that it had some nasty disease or the like) and should not be buried near the house or a watercourse, which it might contaminate. It also makes sense to bury it somewhere out of the way, in an area you won't want to dig over for a flower bed in the future. Make sure the grave is deep enough not to be attractive to badgers, foxes or even your other dogs, with at least 3 feet of soil covering it, and, like Cooper, cover with stones for the first few months, just to be on the safe side.

Bluebell gets her moment in front of the camera, with Jilly Cooper in the pets' cemetery at the end of the garden.

So, practicalities aside, it is down to the nicest ways to remember your beloved companion. Assuming you don't want to wear a locket filled with the ashes of Tibbles or Rover close to your heart (available on Amazon if you do), a little headstone would be a suitable tribute and a marker to future generations that they may find something untoward, should they be planning a garden makeover.

A plant would also be an appropriate memorial, to mark the spot or even just to remind you of your pet if you have chosen for the vet to dispose of the body. It's an easy enough choice if your animal has a suitable name – Damson, Myrtle or Plum, for example – but it could be a rosemary bush, the herb associated with remembrance; a rose bush or other shrub that will flower year after year; or a tree.

A mighty oak may be appropriate for dukes with rolling acres, but a small apple, crab apple, pear or rowan will fit into even a tiny town garden and produce blossom, fruit and colourful foliage through the seasons, working as hard to win your affection as the animal for which it was planted. For my own dogs, an acer or a Tibetan cherry might be more appropriate, as all have rather loud barks.

And finally, back to those souls – well, we will just have to wait and see. Cooper cites a quote ascribed to Martin Luther, the sixteenth-century Protestant reformer, who, when not railing against Catholic corruption and banging his ninety-five theses into a Wittenberg church door, was a great dog-lover: 'Be comforted, little dog,' he told one. 'Thou too in Resurrection will have a little golden tail.'

1 November 2015

Bobbie's headstone was yet to arrive at the time of writing, but will say 'In loving memory, of this bad world, the loveliest and the best'. The big fish in Cooper's pond has, after twenty years of seeing off herons and other fish, finally gone to swim in a celestial pond. He too has been given the honour of a burial and a headstone – 'below Feral the cat, rather inappropriately,' reports Cooper.

LUCIANO GIUBBILEI & FERGUS GARRETT

East Sussex

What makes a garden special, something more meaningful than just a collection of plants in a space? Is it the way it transports you, even for a few minutes, to a world of its own that lingers in the mind when you have left it? That quality, that poetry of place, is something many of us seek.

So it is heartening to hear that even the best in the business can find it elusive: Luciano Giubbilei, a three-time gold-medal winner at Chelsea, has been pondering such questions of late. The Siena-born designer, who is now based in London, has been creating gardens for the past twenty years and

Luciano Giubbilei, in his border in the vegetable garden at Great Dixter. This experimental scheme will have gone by now.

Fergus Garrett and Giubbilei discuss planting schemes in one of Dixter's barns.

has made a highly successful career of it. Drawing on his Italian heritage, he produces formal gardens of clipped hedges, lawns and pleached trees – all very masterful in their use of space and texture, all very cool. All very green, too, with flowers hardly getting a look-in.

Four years ago, however, Giubbilei had come to a crossroads. Without a garden of his own in which to experiment, and with a busy practice to run, as well as projects in America and Europe that kept him constantly on the move, he knew he wanted to find something more in his work, but was unsure which way to turn. Encouraged by the fashion designer Sir Paul Smith to look for inspiration not just in gardens, but in nature, fashion, art, books – wherever there is beauty to be found – and to push himself in a new direction, he decided to ask for help. 'It is about having a conversation and the importance of having that dialogue, finding common ground,' he says.

Among those he contacted was Fergus Garrett, head gardener at Great Dixter, in Northiam, East Sussex. Dixter might seem anathema to Giubbilei's somewhat minimalist approach: an exuberant, ever-changing tableau, brimming with perennial and annual plants set against the background of Edwin Lutyens's formal structure of paths and hedges. The lifetime home of the gardener and author Christopher Lloyd, who died in 2006, it is now run by a trust under the charismatic stewardship of Garrett. Intensely worked, with not a moment that is not observed, tweaked, considered and, if necessary, improved, it is one of the most floriferous gardens in England, as well as among the most famous. It is also a place of learning and mentoring.

When the Italian got in touch in 2011, 'I didn't even know who he was,' admits Garrett, as we all sit with a pot of tea in Dixter's dining room after the day's work in the garden is done. 'Luciano was so honest and open, I thought, "Well, actually, I want to see what's what." You meet people in this game who genuinely want to learn. They are the most rewarding to work with, and you feel like giving them everything. So, when someone shows enthusiasm and passion, you think it is partly your duty to follow it up.'

After meeting and conversing (and both men do like to talk – none of your silent sons of the soil here), Garrett offered Giubbilei a border at the end of the vegetable garden, hard up against a high yew hedge, which would act as a backdrop. Measuring 8 by 50 feet, it would allow him to experiment with various combinations of flowering plants, learning more about their habits and growth. Rachael Dodd and James Horner, two of Dixter's team of gardeners, would work alongside him, helping with the horticultural side of things and looking after it between visits.

Giubbilei has been coming down to Sussex at least once a month over the past four years to play around with plants, but also to observe the way things are done in the garden, to bounce ideas off the others and to open his mind to things he never thought he would accept. 'I never liked variegated plants – I never even looked at them,' he confesses. (He's not alone in this: they are often considered infra dig.) 'Now I have an understanding through conversations with James about the importance of how they bring light if you plant them in groups, and how to group them. I've also learnt how you can make a space architecturally, but you anchor it with plants. That is something I hadn't developed, as it wasn't in my culture, which was about trees and hedges.'

Watching the gardeners at work, and observing their methods and seasonal combinations, has also been useful. 'I want to understand how you put it together.' At first, he tried to put in too much, and things became overcrowded. 'It was asking too much of the space, but there were valid moments,' he says, recalling times of great beauty in the border that were not sustainable in the long run.

His horticultural knowledge – something that designers can be rather lacking in, however good their eye – has deepened through hands-on experience, and his palette has been extended, too. 'It is as if Luciano is in a paint shop,' Garrett says. 'When he is working in the studio, there may be five or six colours he can see, whereas he comes to Dixter and he sees forty, fifty, sixty, a hundred colours.'

It has certainly paid off. With help from Horner (who has since set up his own floristry business), Giubbilei's garden, which included striking ranks of pale yellow 'Chandelier' and 'Cashmere Cream' lupins, stole the show at Chelsea in 2014. Literally, as it won best in show.

So what do those at Great Dixter get out of their designer in residence? 'He has a great feeling for space. We are thinking of the "planty" side – when to sow, when to plant out, how to weave it through, all that kind of stuff,' Garrett says. 'His brain works slightly differently and it has been a positive learning process. He created a beautiful border – the visitors often like it more than ours. They would go, "Who did that border up there?" And I would say, "Oh, I put it together last week!"'

As for Giubbilei, he has written about what he has learnt from his experiences at Great Dixter, and the other influences in his work, as 'a manifesto against stagnation' – something all gardeners could do with thinking about. 'It has been the opportunity of coming to a place. Things have happened that wouldn't have if I had done things in isolation and not taken action.'

He would like to design an English country garden, but recognizes that there is still a journey to travel away from his Italian idiom. 'I think it will happen, but I have to be patient.' For now, he wants to make spaces that will develop over the years, working with the clients towards this – another of his continuing 'conversations'. 'You have to reduce the number of projects, cut down your clients, to be able to focus,' he says. At which Garrett interjects: 'And eventually you get down to one client, which is the best of all!'

15 May 2016

Giubbilei still has an experimental border at Great Dixter, which he visits as often as he can between projects.

At this June moment, parsnip flowers (*Pastinaca sativa*) and *Lupinus* 'Masterpiece' lead the show in the border.

NEISHA CROSLAND

London

Cities are full of surprises. Behind closed doors are treasure troves of individuality and quirkiness, an escape from the uniformity of the streets into a world apart. Approaching Neisha Crosland's home on a quiet road near Clapham Junction, in south-west London, you get an inkling that this might be one of these special places: along the length of the exterior wall runs a *Vitis coignetiae*, the crimson glory vine, its long tendrils trained on parallel wires.

Step through the front door into the broad hallway and the vine is there, too, discreetly fed in through a hole high up in the wall. Out it goes again at the other side of the hall into the large courtyard space, to cover yet another wall, until it eventually comes to ground.

The vine seems almost magical, something you might come across in a book by Roald Dahl, who was Crosland's stepfather from her early twenties. He encouraged her to look at the world through a different prism, taking inspiration from unlikely places, and this has paid off: today she is one of our leading textile designers.

Crosland was a short-sighted child, peering out through a myopic blur. Until the age of eight or so, when spectacles sorted this out, the only way she could see something clearly was to hold it up to her nose to study it closely, as if under a microscope. It gave her a love of the abstraction of shape and detail. Her ideas for patterns often come from flowers and plants, reducing their outlines to a minimalist rendition, then building this up again in layers of colour and line. It was while washing up and staring idly at the winter tracery of her wandering vine, and the outlines of the drainpipes behind it, for example, that the cogs were set into motion for the art-deco-inspired 'Hollywood Grape', one of her most popular designs.

Crosland came to prominence in the 1980s with her bestselling 'Star' collection for Osborne & Little, then in the 1990s she set up under her own name. Her distinctive patterns can be found on a wide variety of materials, from wallpapers to rugs, scarves, folders and even Virago book covers. She now licenses her work through companies such as Turnell & Gigon (which supplies fabrics and wallpapers to interior designers), the Rug Company and Fired Earth.

After you have spent time with her, you start to see pattern everywhere: the cobbles in the courtyard; the way the Aram chairs are arranged like petals around the concrete outdoor table; the parrotia trained in espaliers against the 10-foot-high buttressed back wall. Yet for all her love of colour and ornament, Crosland dresses in sober block colours with little adornment, which belies her cheerful, friendly nature. 'It is a bit of peace and quiet, then you get into a formula – one less thing to think about.'

In the garden, too, instead of blowsy herbaceous borders, she was after something calm and ordered, with plenty of evergreen to maintain interest in winter. She designed the space with Sean Walter, of the Plant Specialist, who is still involved, especially when it comes to pruning the branches of the olive trees. 'I wanted something quite European. I really like the Harold Peto gardens in Wiltshire and the Italian gardens of the Veneto.'

Neisha Crosland, by the Aram chairs neatly arranged around a concrete outdoor dining table.

Enforced by the cocooning walls, which create something of a microcosm, there is an air of a house on the smart outer streets of a prosperous French provincial town, perhaps once having belonged to the local doctor or mayor but now used by a Parisian family for the weekend. The window frames are painted a shade of green reminiscent of Monet's Giverny, and there is an air of quiet permanence about the place, but in fact most of it has been created in phases over the past twenty years.

'This area was bombed quite badly during the war, as Clapham Junction was a target,' Crosland says as we try to work out a way to train a new rambling rose up the buttress that would be acceptably aesthetic to her gimlet eye. 'We think it was once stables that would have served the villas on Wandsworth Common. Then there were eight little houses, which were bombed during the war.'

When she bought the site in 1993, there was a dilapidated 1940s office building in the corner (which is where the green for the windows comes from – she had it matched), a single garage and a large yard, used by a company to store trees and plants for hire.

With the help of an architect, Alex Greenway, the five-bedroom house has expanded over the years, as Crosland's French husband, Stéphane, and sons Oscar, now nineteen, and Samuel, seventeen, turned up. The final phase, completed five years ago, was adding the connecting wing and the office, where she produces two collections a year for a Japanese store.

You would never know it was new, though, such is the unity of the buildings. Walter suggested laying granite cobbles and sandstone flags to connect them, as well as a small lawn. Four huge holm oaks clipped into busby hats stand in regimental formation at the back of the lawn. There were two more, but the automatic watering system went wonky and they died.

Cobbles and sandstone flags give the courtyard garden a feeling of age. You can see the wandering vine trained along the left-hand wall.

The garden is largely monochrome, in shades of green, from the silvery leaves of the olive trees to the glossy foliage of the trachelospermum, which smothers the whole of one wall, along with a kiwi that actually produces fruit. Then there is the chunky outline of a cactus, smuggled back from Sardinia and thriving, and lemon trees that are left out all winter, but still bear fruit. Box is clipped into tight balls or low hedges – 'It is lovely to smell chlorophyll when coming off the street,' Crosland says.

A purple-leaved *Cercis canadensis* 'Forest Pansy', framed by a cube of box hedging, provides a punctuation mark to all this greenery. Elsewhere, 'colour' (i.e., stuff that isn't green) is provided by hydrangeas – both pink and the ghostly white 'Annabelle' – grasses and perennials, such as shapely astrantia, *Geum* 'Tangerine Dream' and geraniums. There are roses, too, for which she has developed a passion since being given a pale yellow 'Roald Dahl' by her mother, Liccy, the writer's second wife. She can remember their names, but jokes it is only because they are newly planted: 'The Generous Gardener' and 'Lady of the Lake'.

Crosland likens the house in its present incarnation to the villas of the ancient Romans, where they would create *rus in urbe* (the countryside in town), with every room facing the inner courtyard, painted with frescoes and centred on a fountain, to remind them of the beauties of the countryside – but with the parties and stimulating conversations that could be somewhat lacking in the provinces.

Judging by the number of wine glasses stacked on the shelves, and the large dining tables and seating areas inside and out, Crosland and her husband follow this merry idea of entertaining. An array of herbs and salads in large zinc containers provides flavouring for the feasts. Then there is the morning after: 'I love washing up, because it is a treat.' She's a glass-half-full kind of girl.

Along with the crimson glory vine to admire as its leaves start turning an autumnal hue, bang in her line of vision when she tackles the dishes is a pretty little pavilion in the courtyard, which cleverly hides the air-conditioning unit. Yet another creamy rose – 'Wollerton Old

Four neatly clipped holm oaks help shield out neighbouring houses.

Hall' – has been planted beside it, replacing a solanum that didn't pass muster. 'It will be nice when the rose climbs on top of that and tumbles down. I just looked at the solanum and thought, "You are so boring."' And that could never be allowed.

4 September 2016

Since the article was written, rose 'Alfred Carrière', Anthriscus sylvestris 'Ravenswing' and more heuchera have made the grade and joined the other plants in the garden. The influence of plants on Crosland's work can be seen in her book Life of a Pattern, *published in 2016.*

CORINNE BAILEY RAE

Leeds

Like many local authorities, Leeds council prides itself on its colourful summer show of annuals, arranged in traditional carpet bedding. A couple of years ago, as the gardeners were renewing the display in a smart suburb of the city, they were asked by a passer-by what was going to happen to the cast-off alyssum and marigolds. Horrified to hear that the plants were destined for the compost heap, she nipped off to her home nearby and returned with a bin liner.

That petite figure with a mass of corkscrew hair, happily shoving the unwanted plants into her bag, was the Grammy-winning singer Corinne Bailey Rae. Although she has sold more than five million records, performed at the White House and supported Stevie Wonder and Lionel Richie, a bag of free marigolds was not to be sniffed at. 'They gave me loads and I put them in the garden – I just wanted to reuse them,' says the singer, who is touring next month to promote her first album for six years, *The Heart Speaks in Whispers*.

Having been away from home for much of the summer, she's embarrassed about the state of her own patch, so it is off limits. We meet instead at the park, where the carpet bedding is now shocking-pink begonias, brightening up a drizzly day. Bailey Rae, who looks at least a decade younger than her thirty-seven years, calls it 'pizza planting'. Nevertheless, she is brimming with enthusiasm for her latest love: gardening. If we hadn't been turfed out of a nearby cafe at closing time, she might still be discussing her favourite roses (she grows 'Grace', 'Ballerina' and 'Wedding Day'), and the joys of her compost heap.

To admit to such a passion is brave, as gardening is an 'old lady' – her words – interest that most people in the music business would keep quiet about (apart from the odd diva demand for a dressing room filled with white orchids). Yet Bailey Rae has no such qualms. She chats happily about making her own rosemary-infused olive oil, which she gives in bottles as Christmas presents, or how much she admires the gardens of Piet Oudolf, the Dutchman who planted the New York High Line and is famous for his late-flowering perennials.

She has modelled a flower bed on a scheme she saw in one of Oudolf's books. 'It is all sorts of reds, as I really like plantings where you have different shapes of the same colour. There are tall things like monarda, rudbeckia and day lilies at the front.

'I haven't got into all the grasses and the prairie-like plants, but what I like is that they don't need a stake. They keep their structure all year and look really beautiful, even after they have lost their colour.'

Bailey Rae – she added the 'Rae' when she married her first husband, Jason Rae, a fellow musician, in 2001 – grew up in Roundhay, in north-east Leeds, where her

Corinne Bailey Rae gamely poses in the pouring rain: not the day for lying on the grass observing plants at close quarters.

mother still lives. 'It is a really green area with tree-lined streets, and she has a front garden and a back garden. Both of them have sloped areas where Mum would do this great staged planting of things that would do well in a dry climate.

'There was a lot of pride. It was a cul-de-sac, so everyone could see everyone else's garden, and all the kids would play out. We had strawberries, blackberries and rhubarb – there wasn't lots, but enough to realize that these things came from the earth and were seasonal.'

Although she can't remember helping her mother much in the garden, Bailey Rae did make a tiny pond with her sisters, Rhea (now an actress in *Coronation Street*) and Candice: 'We just dug out an area and lined it with plastic bags. I am sure it dried out after a week or so, but I remember the frogs coming. It is amazing how quickly nature responds.'

As a girl she loved being outdoors and walking in the nearby Yorkshire Dales, a habit picked up from early outings with her church – but, like many young people, she lost interest while she established her career. She bought her current mid-Victorian four-bedroom house with Jason nine years ago, but they didn't get round to doing anything outside: 'I was so busy and he wasn't really interested in the garden.' It wasn't until his death from an accidental overdose in 2008 that she reconnected with her outdoor space, when she withdrew from the music scene to recover.

One of her great influences over the following years was Janet, the mother of her second husband, Steve Brown, whom she married in 2013. A producer who is also the musical director of her band, he was a friend at the time, and he scooped her up into the embrace of his family in Harrogate.

'I found it really peaceful going to their garden and sitting in their summer house, looking out of the window. Just to have that feeling of time being a lot slower. I would go and see the plant I had watched Janet put in growing, or she would be weeding. She has all the old books and always refers to things by the Latin name, so I try to do that.'

As so many others have found, observing the cycle of nature was a great healer – she has even done a podcast on the subject. 'If you are in an experience when it feels endless and formless, it is good to look out of the window and just notice the small things. It is a really reaffirming thing that time is passing and all that time is healing.'

Bailey Rae's appreciation of nature and its wonders has infiltrated the new album, especially her woozily sexy track *Green Aphrodisiac*, which President Obama had on his summer playlist. It was inspired by lying on the grass and observing plants at close quarters.

Having watched Janet at work in her garden, she wanted the same for her own patch: to be able to look out of her window and see beautiful plants that she had nurtured herself. She had to learn the first rule, though, that gardens aren't static. 'I would be planting and would remark to Janet, "I need to get seven of these." And she would say, "You only need three." Being a young, impatient gardener, I would think, "Oh, there is all this space" – but, of course, now there is just no room. That is what has been the most amazing thing. You plant something and it already looks good, then the wildness takes over.'

One last whiff of the roses before going inside to talk gardening.

Not that Bailey Rae minds. When she moved in, the front of the garden had been concreted over and covered in shale. So she got someone into dig it up and lay a small lawn – although this, too, is being sacrificed bit by bit. 'I got bored of the lawn, then I started to cut in two really big flower beds. I got the shape of them from the smoke bush [*Cotinus coggygria*]. At a certain time of the evening, as the sun is going down, it creates this really long, curved shadow.'

She describes the space as 'an English garden', with formal spaces that work well against the red-brick house, and looser areas full of cottage favourites such as roses, lavender, peonies and hebe. As to whether a smart designer had been in to do a makeover, she looks horrified at the thought. 'Someone comes in and makes sure there are no weeds. I would never get someone in to design it. I want to do it.'

Although Brown usually does the heavy jobs, Bailey Rae tackled some of the hard landscaping herself. 'I flattened it out, got the flags and made the patio – it is homemade-looking. I love that about gardening. You think "I want to improve this", then you decide the shape of the path you want to make, or put these plants in here. You buy things, and they might die, so you think, "OK, that didn't work." You learn from it all.'

The garden has been a refuge from the world and from the demands of touring and performing. One of her favourite places to sit is under the trees. 'There's lots of really nice blossom in May. There's a pear tree and an apple tree, and crab apples that you can make lovely jam with. I like planting things that will last, being around things that will outlive you.' Life in her hidden corner of Leeds goes on.

18 September 2016

Corinne Bailey Rae continues to tour, and to tend her garden.

CATHERINE FITZGERALD
& DOMINIC WEST

London

As a child, Catherine FitzGerald was fascinated by the romantic wildness of the grand gardens in her native Ireland. Daughter of the 29th Knight of Glin – in itself a romantically ancient title, dating back to the fourteenth century — she grew up at Glin Castle, in County Limerick, and had more access than most to these secret places, where exotic species brought back by generations of plant-hunters for the aristocracy would thrive in the temperate air of the Gulf Stream.

'We used to get taken to these wonderful semitropical gardens in Kerry,' she says. Rossdohan, where the house had burnt down in the 1950s, especially made its mark. 'We managed to jump over the wall and get in. It was one of those gardens where huge tree ferns had self-seeded all the way down to the water, and the air is so pure, there were curtains of lichen and massive rhododendrons with cinnamon bark. As a ten-year-old, I was overwhelmed with excitement.'

Those early memories seeded a love of gardens. After leaving Trinity College Dublin, where she read English and art history, FitzGerald trained at the RHS garden at Wisley, in Surrey, for two years, then took a course in historic landscape conservation before joining Arabella Lennox-Boyd, one of the Britain's most distinguished landscape practices, as planting designer.

Today she has her own London firm, and her projects have included her childhood home at Glin, Glenarm Castle, in County Antrim, and Clarendon Park, in Wiltshire, as well as smaller town gardens. She often works with Mark Lutyens, a landscape architect: 'It's a really creative, harmonious partnership.'

That love of the wild also drew her to the house in Shepherd's Bush, west London, where she moved eight years ago. It had belonged to the widow of the actor Brian Glover, with bedsit rooms occupied by thespians and writers. 'Nothing had been done to it for about fifty years,' she recalls. 'It was so magical and the garden was totally overgrown, with raspberries and buddleia. You had to fight your way through to the back.'

The house's hugger-mugger bohemian tradition continues, with the rooms brightly painted, the walls crammed with pictures and Tibetan prayer flags strung up over the kitchen table. On top of the piano sits a dusty Bafta award, for FitzGerald is married to Dominic West, who won it in 2012 for his portrayal of the serial killer Fred West. He is currently baring all in *The Affair*, which returns for a third series next month.

Catherine FitzGerald holds a sceptical Christabel; behind her, Dominic West, who has been lured from his shed at the bottom of the garden.

A comfortable clutter of tender plants on the terrace by the house.

FitzGerald and West have four children: Dora, ten, Senan, eight, Francis, seven, and Christabel, three, who joins us on her return from nursery in a mercurial mood. West's daughter Martha, seventeen, also has a room, and his nephew Henry, who is a scriptwriter, helps with the younger children. 'Before, it was a warren of people living on each floor, and it still is. It is like a big, crazy commune.'

Having sacrificed his study to the boys' bedroom, West now has an office in a black and red shed at the bottom of the garden, which was designed by his wife. It has a stable door to keep small people out, but let fresh air in. One would think he would relish the peace, but FitzGerald says: 'He was going, "I'm banished — I can't even live in my own house!"'

With all those children, including two football-mad boys, the wilderness that FitzGerald so admired has had to be sacrificed for space, although a fig and two huge pear trees remain. Instead, like many a city back garden, it serves the family, with a treehouse, a trampoline and a lawn for kicking a ball around. The last of these is in surprisingly good condition – lush and green, instead of Weetabix brown, after a long summer. This may well be because the family were away on Long Island for the whole of August while West was filming.

Although London's skies tend to be rather greyer than those in New York state, FitzGerald has brought plenty of sunshine into the garden with her use of bold colour, especially near the house. A curved postbox-red bench sits on the terrace near the kitchen's French windows, and it is surrounded by an array of potted plants, including scented-leaf pelargoniums, salvias, abutilons and Japanese anemones. Earlier in the year there were bright lily-flowered tulips and *Geranium palmatum* – 'the best thing ever'. FitzGerald cites Helen Dillon, whom she has known since she was a child, and whose exuberant Dublin garden was one of the most famous in Ireland, as one of her greatest influences. Others are garden designer and writer Mary Keen, and the riotous borders at Great Dixter, in East Sussex.

An espaliered cut-leaf crab apple with little yellow fruits, *Malus transitoria*, provides a screen along the top of a low wall. There is a paulownia in the back corner, which she planted when they moved – it is now huge, its mighty leaves like elephants' ears. Yet she feels a garden without annuals and biennials can be a bit static.

'To really live, you need the biennials, the little surprises – echiums, foxgloves, the poppies that seed everywhere. At Glin, we've got this purple double poppy. Every year it pops up in a huge swathe in a new place and makes all these combinations you never expected.'

London's mild microclimate allows her to grow tender plants that would curl up their toes in chillier parts of the country. She has bananas and melianthus growing in big coloured plastic trugs, with holes drilled in the bottom for drainage (an idea picked up from Dillon; they are easy to move around). These don't need to be taken inside in winter, but can shelter under the pergola, which is swathed in purple and white solanum, along with white *Clematis montana* var *grandiflora*. It is a glorious array. 'I love that slightly sort of clashing, not polite and conventional planting,' FitzGerald says. 'Gardens should be about emotions and feelings. I would rather have the emotion and not be too tidy.'

With a practice to run – not to mention endless school runs – she can't afford to spend too much time tweaking things. Her big project with Lutyens at the moment is the restoration of the grounds at Hillsborough Castle, near Belfast, which is the former governor's residence and the royal family's home when in Northern Ireland. Its upkeep has recently been taken over by Historic Royal Palaces and it is due to open officially in the next couple of years. The aim is to attract 200,000 visitors annually.

'The garden had been ticking over for a long time,' FitzGerald says. 'It's a hundred acres of woods, a lake, a glen, formal parterres, a walled garden that's out of production – it's just grass. I'm thrilled to be doing it. I think I was the right person, as I have so many connections in Ireland. I'm friends with all the head gardeners and we're swapping plants.'

And West, who is home during a break in filming? Eager to leave the limelight to his wife, he lurks in his shed, where I corner him. What does he think of all this flower power? Although he liked gardening as a child, he knows he is beaten and nowadays plays the part of 'the ignorant muscle', cutting the lawn, trimming the box and lopping branches.

He is full of admiration for FitzGerald's knowledge and skills. 'She spends whole afternoons just speaking in Latin. I've known her for a long time – we were at college together, and that was before she was into gardens. I didn't see her for a while, and when I got back with her, all this passion had transformed her. It was one of the most attractive things about her.

'I've never asked her the name of a plant that she doesn't know. I'm slightly envious of her, because we're both lucky in that we both have a passion that will last our whole lives, but I rather feel hers will get better and better, while mine – acting – might diminish.'

The couple have bought an old brewery near Chippenham, Wiltshire, and are in the process of restoring it. As for the garden there, FitzGerald wants to keep it fairly simple, with a sense of the bucolic, blending into the countryside around. Here, West might at last find a leading role: 'This is where I think fruit and veg might be my thing. Hopefully, I will have prize marrows.'

His head gardener is encouraging: 'I'm going to tell him what to do,' FitzGerald says. 'I have great hopes for him.' The local village show had better watch out – there is fresh blood heading for those competition benches.

2 October 2016

FitzGerald's practice is flourishing – among other projects, she and Mark Lutyens are working on a restored physic garden at the Palace of Holyroodhouse in Edinburgh.

ROY LANCASTER
Hampshire

In the morning, when Roy Lancaster opens his bedroom curtains at home in Chandler's Ford, Hampshire, he looks out at a verdant scene, the story of a lifetime of collecting plants across the globe. 'It is like opening the curtains of a theatre. It is a stage, and all these performers – an international cast of plants – they each have something to give me.'

Being a dutiful husband to Sue, his wife of nearly forty years, he goes down to make her a cup of tea and brings it back upstairs. 'Then we sit in bed, drink our tea and plan the day. From our bed we can look out onto the tops of all those trees: the one to the right, the big magnolia in our garden, which fills the sky in April, is a *Magnolia cylindrica*, with white flowers and red fruits and orange seeds that hang on threads. It's wonderful.' He grew it from seed sent over from the Shanghai Botanical Garden; at more than 30 feet, it is now a Champion tree – the largest of its kind in Britain.

Lancaster can also admire the Chilean fire tree (*Embothrium coccineum*), Himalayan dogwood and weeping willow in his neighbour Dot's garden. Beneath the window is a tea tree, *Leptospermum grandifolium*, with silvery grey leaves, and at the bottom of the garden is a *Cornus* 'Porlock', the first tree he planted in the garden, and also 30 feet tall. It bears creamy white flowers in June, followed by an autumn crop of pendulous strawberry-red fruits.

Lancaster will be eighty in December, a fact he would rather I hadn't brought up. 'I don't feel eighty, I can tell you. I am very lucky in that instead of throwing away childish things and growing up, I only have to start talking about plants and my energy levels rise.' And indeed he talks with such unabashed enthusiasm for the various species in his garden, and the adventures he has had over his long life of looking for local flora in far-flung places such as China, New Zealand, Chile and Malaysia, he could still be the keen fourteen-year-old boy who paid 2*s*. 6*d*. of his pocket money to become a junior member of the Bolton Field Naturalists' Society.

Even after more than fifty years of living in the south, Lancaster retains his flattened Lancashire tones, which are instantly recognizable to gardeners of a certain age from his BBC broadcasts on *Gardeners' Question Time* and *Gardeners' World*. He is also a prolific plant explorer, lecturer and writer, and one of horticulture's grandees – holder of a Veitch Memorial Medal and the Victoria Medal of Honour, the Royal Horticultural Society's highest honours, as well as both an OBE and a CBE for services to horticulture. President of various august horticultural societies, he has just written *My Life With Plants*, as the name would suggest, the autobiography of his long relationship with plants.

Daphne bholua 'Peter Smithers', named after the plantsman who originally collected its seed from Nepal.

Lancaster's recall for these plants and where they come from would put an elephant to shame, yet there's no trace of the impatience with those less knowledgeable that you sometimes find with true plantsmen. He would rather share his passion than use it as a weapon of condescension, and for the past twenty years or so he has been inviting groups of horticultural students to the garden for study days, with Sue feeding them tea and homemade cakes.

It takes him back to his early years of interest in plants, when he was encouraged by mentors who were the age he is now. Life has come full circle: 'You see an interest developing and you want to fan the flames.' So, 'If I was asked, "What is your greatest achievement in life?", certainly in my job it has been encouraging young people.'

When the Lancasters bought their red-brick late-Victorian house in 1982, Roy had just left Sir Harold Hillier's famous arboretum near Romsey (now called the Sir Harold Hillier Gardens and run by Hampshire county council), where he had worked initially in the nursery, then for ten years as its first curator. Although he is always welcome back and remains a patron, 'It was no longer mine; I had regarded it as my big garden.'

He needed somewhere to observe various plants he had collected, been given or just wanted to try out. The couple's first home had been near Winchester prison, where he had gardened on chalk in a tiny space. To Lancaster, the soil wasn't the problem it is to many gardeners, but the garden was full and he was keen to try out the likes of rhododendrons, azaleas and camellias, which would turn their toes up in those alkaline conditions.

They were told about the four-bedroom house, with a third of an acre of garden, and came to have a look. 'The house looked awful, inside especially,' Lancaster remembers, although he was more interested in what could be done outdoors. 'There was nothing in the garden you could call an interesting ornamental plant, except for three *Magnolia liliiflora* 'Nigra'. They stood out for their quality. There were some scabby apple trees that were dying and some soft fruit. Nothing else.'

As for the soil, the north-facing front garden, which is a large enough space for there to be lots of sun as well as shade nearer the house, is acidic sand over gravel and very well drained. 'It's the nearest you can get in cultivation to the Gobi desert in summer; water doesn't hang around at all,' Lancaster says, with an excitement for such conditions that few could summon. It was the perfect place for the acid-loving plants he had been so missing, and would later become a home too for Mediterranean ones, which hate sitting with wet feet. The back of the house was south-facing on clay, with a bare wall on which to grow sun-loving climbers.

They decided to go for it. While Sue got on with improving the interiors, Roy was in charge of the garden. The magnolias are still there; however, he failed to follow the advice that he would give others – to wait a while in order to clear and prepare the space, then plan how you would populate it with some idea of an overall design. There were two truckloads of plants to accommodate, including many he had collected in China ('the mother of British gardens, where most of the species are found') and Russia, and they had been sitting in a friend's garden, waiting for a new home. They needed to get in the ground as soon as possible.

One idea he did have, though, was to divide the back garden into quarters, with two sections for plants from China and Japan, and another for miscellaneous species, including those from the Himalayas. 'The remaining quarter down at the bottom, I had that for several rows of seedlings, and I managed to grow vegetables.' However, the veg were too much like hard work, and he needed the ground for his precious ornamentals, so they were sacrificed.

Roy Lancaster finds a place to pose among the thousand or so plants in the garden.

So, too, was the original scheme. 'Eventually the idea of having two quarters for China didn't really work, because I had lots of other things I wanted to grow and there was no space,' he explains. So the populations have migrated somewhat into each other's territory; but Lancaster makes a note of every move. 'I have always kept a ledger recording every planting, dates, origin, who, when and where it has gone here. I've labelled every border and bed, so I know exactly where I have planted it, should I lose the label.' As he now has coming up to a thousand plants in the garden, it certainly helps.

The long-running garden show isn't over yet, though: the couple are off to Malta this month, to look at the plant life there. Somehow one feels that a few new members will be joining the cast at Chandler's Ford soon.

5 March 2017

Roy and Sue still travel with unabated enthusiasm to check out the plants and birds of the world.

KELLY BROOK

Kent

Kelly Brook wants me to admire her neatly trimmed box and inspect her brassicas. For the actress and model, who was once voted the sexiest woman alive by readers of FHM magazine, and who attracts double entendres like bees to a honeypot, has been bitten by the gardening bug.

As well known for her generous curves and racy calendars as for appearances on TV shows such as *Strictly Come Dancing*, Brook has been hard at it for the past ten years. Ever since she bought her fifteenth-century Wealden farmhouse and surrounding five acres in Kent, she has been discovering the joys of getting down and dirty in the flower beds. She actually knows her stuff, but only recently has she been sharing her passion with her million-plus followers on social media.

She has sold most of her designer frocks, closed her London bar, and these days is as likely to post pictures of oxeye daisies at sunset or her immaculately tidy potting shed, as images of herself squeezed into a revealing outfit – to the dismay of some of her more ardent admirers.

They will be disappointed, too, that her smoulderingly handsome fiancé, Jeremy Parisi, also a model and actor, makes frequent appearances in her posts, between the hollyhocks and the box hedges. He lives in Paris but makes good use of the Eurostar, and is at the house when I visit, lurking indoors while we talk gardens until we all sit down to a lunch of chicken pie and salad from the veg patch.

This is a rare invitation. It is the first time Brook has allowed a print publication through the gates, and she's a little wary. She guards her privacy fiercely and is firmly in control of images on her home turf. 'It's OK being a sexy calendar girl, but you are only connecting at one level,' she says. 'I am actually revealing more here than I did on the calendar.'

All this care over getting the perfect picture of a trug full of peas, or nonchalantly parking her old-fashioned Pashley bike in front of the herbaceous borders, marks what she hopes will be a new career direction. 'Most of my TV work is celebrity-orientated, but I watch and love things like *Gardeners' World*. I would love to be on something that shows my passion for gardening.'

She first saw her Grade-II-listed farmhouse when she was working in Los Angeles. 'I got so bored of not having any seasons, never seeing any change,' she recalls as we sit in the sunshine drinking coffee on the cobbled terrace, with birdsong filling the air. 'It was like living in a car park – it was concrete everywhere.' So she started to trawl the internet. 'I am from this area, my family live locally and it was a bit of a whim, really. I was earning money and I thought, "I need to invest it in something that will be my forever home."'

Brook is clearly not just a pretty face: after she won a beauty contest in her teens her career took off, and by the time she was nineteen she was investing in property. 'When you are acting and stuff, you get a lot of time off,' she says. 'I was always buying properties, renovating them and selling them on. I had done three in LA and a couple in London. My job is really paying for my hobby, but luckily my hobby was lucrative at the time, because house prices were going up and up.' Brook would throw herself into the renovations. 'My family like working with our hands – my great-grandfather was a piano-maker, my grandfather was a gardener and my dad was a scaffolder. I have definitely got that in my genes. I like making things, digging and planting.'

The property had once been an apple and pear farm, and there are remnants of the old orchard at the top of the hill behind the house. As for the gardens, the previous owners left well-established 'bones' – including a lime walk, a laburnum arch, a swimming-pool area and a pond – though she had to remove a clutter of overgrown plants to reveal them.

Her first job was to get rid of the thick leylandii boundary hedge. 'It was so dark,' she says. 'You didn't see any sky, you didn't see any indigenous trees in the background. Now we have sun, and all the roses and plants do so much better.'

We walk round to the other side of the house and look at the grassy slopes leading up to the lime walk, which are dotted with yew and rounded box topiary. Her years in front of a camera have given her a good eye for the bigger picture: she sees the garden as a whole rather than merely focusing on discrete areas. 'You couldn't even see the lime walk before,' she says. 'These yew hedges that look like little soldiers going up the hill – they were a mess. I clipped them down to the bare trunk. I didn't think they'd ever grow back, but they did. It took about five years and now they are really manageable.'

What of the lime walk itself? 'I've created a spring bank there, with lots of daffodils, crocus and hellebores.' Brook also cleared the brambles from the sloping woodland behind the house so the bluebells could flourish, and seeded foxgloves, oxeye daisies and poppies to come later. 'I like the idea that, as you walk around, everywhere has a different vibe,' she says.

Around the house are cottage plants such as *Alchemilla mollis*, lupins, irises, lavender and foxgloves, with dahlias, hollyhocks, anemones and rudbeckias to come. Someone comes in to help with the mowing and heavy work, but Brook swears she does all the planting herself, and picks up ideas from gardens she has visited. She's also been planting up old galvanized bathtubs in different styles, as well as little crates of wild flowers, inspired by the meadows at Great Dixter.

Then there are the masses of roses: covering the walls of the house; lining the flagstone path; filling the box parterre. When put on the spot, Brook can't remember all the names, but there is one she never forgets – the blush-pink 'Maid of Kent', covering an arch – how could she not have that?

Fresh as a daisy: Kelly Brook reveals her love of gardening.

Whether or not she gets to be a green-fingered TV goddess, Brook has made her own gardener's world at the farmhouse and is obviously enjoying the new direction it is taking her in. The place is more than a mere base, however. 'As much as it was a cute little cottage I always dreamt about having, this is now our family home,' she says. 'It is a place that captured that moment in time when my dad had been diagnosed with cancer and my brother had been posted to Afghanistan. There was so much turmoil in my life and the world, and this home really grounded me. "If everything just goes to pot," I thought, "I've got a home, I can grow vegetables, and I have an orchard and I have my own water – we have everything we need as a family." That is the underlying emotional connection with the house.' It is up at the top, with views over the Kent Weald, that she loves most. There's a shepherd's hut and a fire pit, and she's been sowing new wildflower areas. 'My dad passed away about eight months after I moved in. He loved the orchard and I feel his spirit is here with me. For us as a family, when we spend time up there, it reminds us of him – I walk around there and I feel closer to him.'

2 July 2017

Brook continues to post pictures of her garden on social media. My own Instagram picture of her smelling a daisy had twenty thousand hits, though most of the young men who started following me after that seem to have dropped away.

The fifteenth-century farmhouse is surrounded by cottage-style planting.

INTRODUCTION TO PART TWO

As with gardening, writing about gardens is a pleasurable task that never ends; there is always another path to walk along, another plant to encounter for the first time (and then to notice in every subsequent garden one visits), another way of thinking about how to approach a space. The following are encounters with generous gardeners that I had during the time when I was putting together this book. Because of the necessity of having to return to my computer on a regular basis, most of them are within a hundred miles of my home in the West Country: how lucky to have such a rich variety of gardens so – nearly – on my doorstep! One, however, is as far away as Tangier . . .

Low evening light at Yews Farm, Martock.

PENELOPE HOBHOUSE

Somerset

I first met Penelope Hobhouse in 2002, at her converted coach house in Bettiscombe, Dorset. Rather nervous of coming to interview one of horticulture's grandest of *grandes dames* on the publication of her new book, *The Story of Gardening*, I drove down the track to the house with trepidation, all names of even the most common of plants or important milestones in the history of landscape flying out of my head like pigeons released from a coop.

Such nerves were quickly dispelled, and I was welcomed as if I were a trusted – and rather more knowledgeable than I was at that stage – friend. As she poured tea from a silver pot in the glass-walled drawing room, we talked about how she was going to scale down the courtyard garden we looked out upon. This she had created from scratch over the nearly ten years she had lived there: the idea, in preparing for her later years, was to reduce the high-maintenance perennials and to rely instead on shrubs and self-seeders. 'In the end it will be topiary shapes of grey and green. By the time I am eighty, I will still be able to cope.'

Hobhouse is now well past that milestone, still very much coping, and spending several hours a day in the garden. But since we first took tea together and have indeed become friends (there have been many such occasions since; lunches too – she is an excellent cook – plus a jolly trip together around the gardens of the Italian lakes), she has moved house twice and has created two more gardens. So much for winding down.

Despite being one of the world's most distinguished garden designers – she has been awarded the Victoria Medal of Honour, the Royal Horticultural Society's highest accolade, and an MBE for services to gardening – Hobhouse was a late starter, career-wise. Having graduated in Economics from Girton College, Cambridge, in 1951, she married Paul Hobhouse the next year and produced three children. In 1967, they came to live at Hadspen House in Somerset, which had been in his family since the eighteenth century. Here, untrained but eager to learn, she threw herself into restoring the neglected eight acres of gardens, as the family wanted to return it to their Edwardian grandmother's day. 'I gardened all the time and planted trees and shrubs just to cover the ground and had to use weedkillers and mulch to conquer established ground elder and bindweed; at that time, I hardly thought of perennials or bulbs,' she remembers. She also became fascinated by garden history and design.

In 1979 she and her second husband, John Malins (who died in 1992), took over as tenants of Tintinhull House, a National Trust property near Yeovil, where they remained for fourteen years. They renovated the garden, keeping in mind

Penelope Hobhouse, who continues to work several hours a day in her garden.

the spirit of Phyllis Reiss, who had created a magical garden there during the 1940s and 1950s, before leaving it to the National Trust in 1959. Their work was a success and visitor numbers rose from two thousand a year to twenty thousand by the time they left in 1993.

It was during her time at Tintinhull that her design career took off too, fuelled by the publication of *Colour in Your Garden*, in 1985 (there were many more books to follow, written with an academic rigour not always apparent in gardening books). She made gardens for the Queen Mother at Walmer Castle, Kent, the RHS Garden at Wisley, Aberglasney in Carmarthenshire and for the fashion designer Jil Sander, in Germany. She was especially popular in America and had many clients there, including Steve Jobs, the founder of Apple, for whom she made an English cottage garden in Palo Alto, California (Niall, her son, had to tell her who Jobs was). As clients in America multiplied, she discovered – as every designer will tell you – that the more you charge, the more inclined clients are do what they are told. 'If you are not charging at all, they just do what they like after you have finished and that is very upsetting.'

The formality of Italian gardens has been a great influence on her style and, over the years, she also became fascinated with those of Islam – envisaged as 'a foretaste of heaven to come'; until she was eighty she would take tours to Iran

Alliums, honesty and euphorbia provide zing on a rainy May day.

and India. When I revisited Bettiscombe in 2008, as she was selling up to move back to a stable flat at Hadspen, then owned by Niall, she was researching for a book on the history of Mughal gardens. It was never finished, as so much had to be read in translation and there was too much cross-checking of complicated names and places to do – Hobhouse is not one for mistakes in such details. 'I was exhausted.' However, the travel and research involved had been worth it in themselves.

Instead, she made a small garden at her new home at Hadspen, as well as keeping hens and tending to a large glasshouse filled with tender plants. However, with the estate about to be sold, she moved yet again, in 2011, to an L-shaped former dairy barn and milking parlour in nearby Pitcombe, the 70-foot-long garden enclosed by the buildings and hedging. Here, the former owner allowed her to start work on the garden even before the sale had gone through. It was a

Looking from the new wild garden, over a bridge perfectly aligned with the path, towards the house.

generous gesture, especially considering that the first thing Hobhouse did was weedkill the lawn. 'It saved me months,' she says.

With the sale completed, Hobhouse then added mulch to the top of the dead sod: there was to be no high-maintenance grass here, only wide beds and four straight paths. A central path leads from the entrance gate, which is framed with *Akebia quinata*, to a flagstoned terrace and the front door. For the first year or two, it was hard work to dig through the underlying sod, but, nearly five years after she moved in, 'it's really easy to work.' She also hadn't taken into account that it had been a cow yard, with the richest of soil as a consequence: 'I went on feeding and mulching it because that is what we do as gardeners. And now everything is huge.'

Her approach has been much the same as it was at Bettiscombe. 'I was trying to prepare for my old age and not being as fit as I am, luckily, still – more or less.

That was very important: to plan it in sequence of how it would develop and be less work every year.' The garden is very sheltered, which gives her the opportunity to grow many tender plants. 'The other thing I wanted to do was to experiment growing my favourite shrubs and small trees. I also grow perennials, which are self-seeders, among them many umbellifers.' Non-woody plants include peonies, hellebores, honesty, eryngiums, white rosebay willow herb and many cranesbills. Favourites are *Smyrnium perfoliatum* and angelica.

Small trees and shrubs are planned to create areas of light and shade, and to control the architecture of the garden. She gives me a list: glossy leaved phillyreas, June-flowering hoherias from New Zealand, *Acacia pravissima*, Iranian elms (grown from seed brought back from a tour), *Salix magnifica*, *Malus hupehensis* and *Heptacodium miconioides*. Smaller shrubs include *Bupleurum fruticosum*, tree peonies and daphnes. As the woody plants grow, they will push out the perennials and gradually simplify the garden. 'It is planned so that if I am in a wheelchair or whatever happens mentally, it won't need very much work and I won't have to watch it deteriorating because the main plants will always survive.'

Hobhouse also takes cuttings of many salvias (mainly blue) and grows annuals to put in her thirty pots placed to frame the paths around the garden – *Nicotiana langsdorfii* and *N. mutabilis* are favourites. You would think that would be enough to keep her occupied; it is a lot of pots to water in summer. But, through the gate she could see the bottom of a railway embankment on the opposite side of a narrow stream, covered in neglected woodland and brambles, which rankled. So Niall bought it, and she has made a wild garden of native trees and shrubs to enhance the view. A little bridge across to it is aligned on the central path of the original garden.

At Pitcombe she says she has created her first truly selfish garden. 'When I did Bettiscombe, I knew my clients would come and see it. Now I don't have any of these feelings at all and in a funny way it has been a great release. The other thing is that the plants protect me from the outside world. I am a sort of recluse in a way, and I feel protected.'

17 May 2017

Penelope Hobhouse is currently working on a revised edition of The Story of Gardening, *the book I first went to see her about.*

Ranks of white rosebay willowherb and self-seeded opium poppies behind *Bupleurum fruticosum* in June.

TESSA TRAEGER
& PATRICK KINMONTH

Devon

In the small farmyard at Cory Manor in north Devon is an outbuilding with a slate roof so mossy, buckled and bowed that you fear it might not make it to the end of the day without collapsing. But of course it does, as it has for hundreds of years, a reminder of the long life of the manor, which was originally built in the thirteenth century, with additions, remodelling and restorations over the centuries since.

The shed is rather a metaphor for the way Tessa Traeger and Patrick Kinmonth have lived at Cory Manor over the past thirty years: keeping the place as true to its medieval spirit as possible but propped up with the discreet addition of twenty-first-century comforts. There may be underfloor heating and wifi but you won't find cereal packets on open shelves in the pantry, nor a widescreen telly stuck on a wall; instead each nook and cranny is as carefully arranged as a Vermeer painting, the interiors hung with faded tapestries, the antique furniture proudly bearing the scuffs and scrapes of its history.

That the place should be thus, the *mise en scène* of lives in which the visual takes precedence, should come as no surprise, as both Traeger and Kinmonth have made their considerable reputations from their keen eyes. Traeger's striking photographic portraits, still lifes, gardens and landscapes, often shot in black and white, are instantly recognizable, and she is still working hard on exhibitions and books, most recently illustrating Stewart Grimshaw's *The Loveliest Valley: A Garden in Sussex*, with another, on the private gardens at Petworth House, in the pipeline.

Kinmonth was a precociously young arts editor when they met in the 1980s at *Vogue*, and they worked together on many projects there over the years. Their most notable collaboration outwith Vogue House was in 2003, on *A Gardener's Labyrinth*, both an exhibition of Traeger's portraits of the leading names in gardening of the day at the National Portrait Gallery, and a thoughtful accompanying book, written by Kinmonth.

Nowadays their work has taken divergent paths. Kinmonth turns his hand with equal aplomb to opera and ballet direction, costume and set design. He also writes, paints, designs interiors and curates fashion exhibitions, most recently 'Vogue 100: A Century of Style' and 'House Style: Five Centuries of Fashion at Chatsworth'.

Traeger makes the long journey to north Devon from their flat in London about once a month and stays for ten days or so (they both have studios here). I am lucky to catch Kinmonth on a rare weekend at home, as he admits that his candle is burning 'consistently throughout, not just at both ends'. He is currently in the middle of directing *Tannhäuser* in Cologne, and later in the week he is flying out to Hungary to discuss a new project.

On a warm July day we have lunch in the open-sided 'go down', the outdoor dining room in a former stable a few hundred yards from the house. People tell the couple how lucky they are to have found it in such a picturesque condition, with the original river-cobbled floor and bits of eighteenth-century plastering still showing, or suck their teeth about how much there is still to do to make it smart, without realizing the painstaking work that has gone into making it like this. 'These are the things that have the ghosts of the people and the place embedded in them,' says Kinmonth.

A gardener comes in three days a week, and the caretaker also works as the groundsman, but Traeger describes herself as 'head gardener', taking care of planning and ordering; and she also loves

Patrick Kinmonth and Tessa Traeger seeking a 'destination'.

the process of sowing seeds and pricking out and potting on. Today Kinmonth is playing the supporting act and, despite his relentless workload, he has prepared smoked salmon trout and vegetables from the garden as if he has all the time in the world. For such an artistic maestro, he is somewhat disappointingly dressed in a T-shirt and shorts: I had hoped for at least a three-piece linen suit. Traeger is looking rather more satisfactorily the bohemian part, dressed in a French peasant's smock of rough linen and wearing a wide-brimmed straw hat, while Whistler the lurcher drapes himself elegantly on a bench behind us.

We look out over a changing array of pots arranged by the go down (pelargoniums at this time of year). Beyond, stages in the property's history are acknowledged and celebrated in a layered landscape developed over the centuries. 'A lot of trees were planted in 1900 – the copper beech, wellingtonias, fir trees and so on,' says Traeger. A western red cedar was blown down in the great storm of 1989 and a dozen or so rhododendrons were revealed and began to blossom. One has reached 40 feet. There's also a giant *Magnolia* x *soulangeana*, a hybrid first bred in France in 1820. 'It is absolutely sensational.' The 'Avalanche' crab apples – which are the same pink as the magnolia – come out at the same time, as do *Tulipa* 'Clusiana', which have naturalized in the grass underneath. 'So that is an amazing moment. Patrick being a theatre designer,

Cory Manor, seen from across the pond surrounded by native plants.

there is a great deal of "curtain up" going on here,' she says, and 'moments' are mentioned frequently. Tulips, for example, are arranged in pots, where the pelargoniums are now, and get their moment. 'I like to have each part of the garden looking fabulous for a short time, so I can photograph it, and then when it's over I move on to another area. Things dotted about doesn't work as it doesn't make a good photograph.'

'Destinations' is another favourite word; somewhere to walk to during a particular area's moment – say, the spring wild daffodils in an upper field, or the wildflower meadows in May and June. We follow a path through the woods to a tiny shack – an inviting destination during the bluebells' moment – and squeeze in, Whistler included. We sit on the narrow wooden benches to admire it, like three Alices in Wonderland after munching Eat Me cake, Kinmonth's head almost reaching the ceiling.

Borders near the house are planted to flower in September to attract butterflies, and are coming into their own with the rich jewel colours of asters, salvias and heleniums, and there is a whole plantation across the lane devoted to buddleia for the same purpose. Another destination/moment/act is a herb garden that looks its best in May and June (Traeger and Kinmonth are not so strict on what counts as a herb nowadays), the colour-themed beds protected from the sea winds by being planted within the walls of a former barn. It is cobbled with pebbles brought up in their pockets from the River Torridge at the far end of the property, as they return from their G&T destination by its bank of an evening.

Their travels to other gardens have been a great influence. By a shady wall of the house is a collection of ferns, inspired by Alan Bloom, the great Norfolk nurseryman, whom Traeger photographed for *A Gardener's Labyrinth*; huge hydrangeas are in full glory at the time of my visit, as is a kitchen garden using raised beds (copied from Penelope Hobhouse's garden in Bettiscombe, Dorset); the old vegetable patch has been turned into a cutting garden inspired by that at Château Lafite in the Médoc, as the clay soil of the area had yielded such disappointing results veg-wise.

The couple share their land with the local wildlife with a good grace, and even go out of their way to encourage it, rather than fighting the constant battle for control that many gardeners wage. 'My *raison d'être* is that our place is a kind of nature reserve; we have twenty-five acres, five of which we garden; the rest is farmed by our neighbour,' says Traeger. The previous owner had fenced off the bottom of the 'garden' area to keep out the deer, but they have introduced a series of shallow terraces, so the two meld into each other and the sightline from the house through to the fields and trees beyond is not broken. 'We were going to make a ha-ha but we were advised that the local deer are very nervous and don't actually come into the garden.'

Below the terraces they have dug a pond, modelled on one at a house they used to rent near Aix-en-Provence and planted with yellow flag irises and other natives. Their efforts have paid off, as there is a thriving population of frogs, slow worms, grass snakes, dragonflies and butterflies, and more than a hundred species of birds have been recorded on the land.

There is one sort of wildlife they are not so keen on: molluscs. 'Because of the high rainfall we have a massive slug and snail problem. We are organic, so we can't use slug pellets,' says Traeger. Instead, their defence against the slimy invaders is to introduce plants that are off the mollusc menu – and over the years finding these has become something of a sport. Traeger reels off her allies in battle: thalictrum, veronicastrum, snapdragons, salvias, asters, comfrey, all kinds of sedums, nasturtiums, tulips, sweet william, zinnias, rhododendrons, hydrangeas, roses, penstemons and ferns. Hopeless here are lupins, delphiniums, dahlias, love-in-a-mist and sunflowers.

I ask Traeger if there are any areas of creative tension between two people with such firm views on what is aesthetically acceptable (even the plastic tomato growbags are covered with a faded red Laura Ashley fabric, left over from an advertising shoot). There is a slight stand-off about how many brambles should be allowed to remain in the wilder bits for the nesting birds (Kinmonth would prefer fewer), but generally they are in accord. 'I know what he likes and he knows what I like. We've worked together for years on all sorts of different projects, so we are quite used to the give and take of a creative relationship. It is not a problem for us.'

Here in this quiet corner of Devon, far from the madding crowd, harmony reigns.

24 July 2017

LOUISE DOWDING

Somerset

Louise and Fergus Dowding moved to Yews Farm in Martock, Somerset, in 1996, seduced by the warm honey tones of the seventeenth-century house and its mullioned windows, the high walls and the farm buildings on the enclosed three-quarters of an acre site. The excellence of the soil in the area had also been one of the draws, but that didn't turn out quite as planned. 'What we didn't know is that there had been a lot of farm buildings which had been knocked down, so the soil is extremely thin. It should be fantastic but it's not,' says Louise.

There was, however, a large enough area of deep, delicious loam for Fergus to grow the vegetables that keep the family supplied all year, while Louise got on with making her garden. The division between the two is strict: 'We are very separate and have our own kingdoms, otherwise it would be divorce material,' she insists.

In corroboration of this, as we are talking about flowers rather than fancy veg, Fergus slinks off to his study to peruse his seed catalogues. Louise and I are sitting sinking a glass of wine in the large conservatory they built in 2010, to make the most of the view of the garden on wet days (there are plenty of those in Somerset), and to protect their collection of rather rude cacti. The wine bottle is all ours.

We have been friends since we met at a party in a freezing tent on top of a hill in February 1999. Fergus was wearing one of his natty and extremely loud checked suits, Louise was dressed in her grandmother's fur tippet and a dressing-up-box tiara. They looked like fun, and when I learned she was also a garden designer, I invited myself round for an inspection. Even in winter, and although it was only a few years old, the garden was already showing precocious signs of being a grown-up.

Yews Farm shows just how much fashions change, even in gardening. When the couple moved in there was an established vegetable patch, pretty much where it is now, but almost everything else had to go: a couple of shallow ponds lined with fertilizer sacks, curving borders laid out and cut along the lines of a hosepipe, and a rose pergola down the centre of the garden – it looked like something straight out of the 1975 *Reader's Digest Illustrated Guide to Gardening*. However a beautiful old pear tree, large enough to sit under, was given a reprieve, although its fruit is as hard as diamonds and fit only for cooking.

Louise trained as a sculptor and landscape designer, before working as an assistant to Penelope Hobhouse. She now has her own garden design business. So she approached the layout methodically, drawing out a grid plan of borders and grassy paths, with a terrace near the house. Among the first things to go

Louise Dowding gets stuck into cutting the topiary. Behind is the old pear tree, the only relic of the previous garden.

in were box balls to delineate the end of each of Fergus's vegetables beds, and to give some winter interest. When they later grew too large, they were moved to the ornamental garden, where they are now cut to resemble segments of an orange, as the balls were too bulky. She also planted a group of bay trees at the back of the garden; they are pruned into open umbrella shapes by Fergus. 'What I wanted was Levens Hall,' says Louise. 'I'm nearly there; just give me another hundred years.'

When the box was moved to the ornamental borders, it replaced the carex and miscanthus Louise had originally planted, inspired by beautiful photographs of Piet Oudolf's dreamy, drifting landscapes of perennials and grasses, their fronds sparkling with frost on a crisp winter day. They could look wonderful – which is how I remember them – but were not to last. Louise explains: 'In 1996, grass gardens were extremely popular, but it didn't work here. In the winter, when they were supposed to look fantastic, they didn't: it was just dead and dull. It was too wet, too grey. I decided that with the grasses it was six/seven months of nothingness and they left far too many blanks. It's not a big garden, everything needs to work all the time.'

A quince 'Meeches Prolific' – in this case a misnomer. 'It hasn't produced anything for years,' says Dowding. 'Its days are numbered.'

The terrace, where the family spends a lot of time during the summer, shaded by *Crataegus* x *lavallei* 'Carrierei' and *Crataegus prunifolia*.

The grasses went off to be burnt in the farmyard beyond the garden but the seedlings still appear through cracks in the concrete surface, happier there than in the borders. They catch the low evening light as they should, and sway along with *Verbena bonariensis*. 'Nature is making its own arrangement,' says Louise. 'They look much better down there.'

Nature is also displaying its innate artistry in a gravel area to the side of main garden, which is almost entirely self-seeded, with thalictrum, hollyhocks, *Eryngium* 'Miss Willmott's Ghost', eglantine rose and aquilegia (and more) mingling with umbellifers such as *Ligusticum lucidum*, parsnips and fennel to create something of a dry jungle. What interests Louise here is what comes up and where. In the main garden she pretty much knows what is going to appear, as she has planned it. Here though, 'I am never quite sure what is going to happen.'

It's all in-your-face stuff, rather like the towering *Echium pininana*, cardoons and stooled *Paulownia tomentosa* in an enclosed courtyard, once a poison garden, but tamed somewhat since the advent of children (their daughters, Agnes and Octavia, are now teenagers). Louise is not one for miniature jewels. 'I'm a tall person,' she says. 'I don't want to be scrabbling around on the ground.'

Hydrangea paniculata 'Limelight', with some of the overgrown box balls, now dissected like orange segments.

Rather than focusing on individual plants, she is concerned about the overall picture, especially on days too wet or cold to go outside, when you can only look at it from the house. With bumpy box hedges hiding the vegetable garden – wonderful and abundant in summer; not so attractive as bare earth in winter – and a revolving display of pots on the terrace, there is a considered structure of greenery throughout the year.

I suggest that what interests her is creating a stage, on which the plants play their part as chorus or leading players, but Louise thinks that too trite. 'It is much more fundamental. When I come in here, there is a sense of absolute peace, of serenity, even though I know I have gone through physical anguish to get to that point. It is a haven, which is all walled, so nobody looks over you.' And will she ever be able to throw herself back on the deep conservatory sofa and say her job is done? 'It is never finished; next year will always be better. The aim is to reach a state of visual perfection. I know I will never achieve it but that is what keeps you driving on. That is part of the pleasure.'

10 July 2017

MICHAEL
LE POER TRENCH

Somerset

Ionce asked a wealthy owner of a beautiful garden whether he ever dug in with his staff and worked in the borders. A shudder came over him at the thought of engaging in something so menial. 'I point,' he replied, rather crisply. That was as near to the soil as he got.

Michael Le Poer Trench could well afford to be a pointer too; after all, his partner, Sir Cameron Mackintosh, is the world's most successful theatrical impresario, and they employ three full-time gardeners to work on the twelve-acre garden surrounding Stavordale Priory in Somerset. Instead, it is rare to see him out of work trousers, a secateur holster strapped round his waist, and wearing the slightly distracted air of someone itching to get back to his pruning.

The couple have lived at Stavordale since 1992. An Augustinian priory built in the thirteenth century, it became a farm after the dissolution of the monasteries and was remodelled in the nineteenth century as a gentleman's residence. The architect used for this was Thomas Collcutt, who by neat coincidence also designed the Palace Theatre in London's West End, where Mackintosh's production of *Les Misérables* made its debut in 1985 (it is still going strong). But it was David and Georgia Langton, from whom they bought the place, who had made the greatest impression on the garden. A designer by profession, Georgia laid out the 'bones' of much of what is here today, including two cloister areas, a large potager, an orchard, and borders and a formal lawn by the house. The tightly clipped yew columns, standard Portuguese laurels, and box hedges and blobs that have reached maturity now are all down to her, and ensure there is always a strong framework, whatever the season.

At the time they moved to Stavordale Le Poer Trench was working as a theatrical photographer, but over the years his role has morphed into being that of director, designer and producer of the gardens. Under his aegis the potager has been extended, and new greenhouses built; a meadow area and birch walk planted, the trunks of the *Betula jacquemontii* (pressure-washed in spring to keep them brighty-white) underplanted with foxgloves, daffodils and *Brunnera macrophylla* 'Jack Frost'; the lake has been dredged and expanded, another lake created and a boathouse built; and a tiered rill added at the top of the formal lawns. The apple trees that flank it can be lit from underneath for dramatic night-time effect.

There is always work in progress. Jez Stamp, who won the Institute of Horticulture's Young Horticulturist of the Year award in 2013, joins the full-time gardeners twice a week and he and Le Poer Trench are rethinking the formal upper cloister garden, which is enclosed by high, chamfer-edged box hedges and has a stone fountain at its centre. The colour scheme is mixed pink, white and blue but it would make the perfect place for a white garden. 'I thought, let's give it a go,' says Le Poer Trench. White veronicastrum, *Calamintha nepeta* 'White Cloud' and *Thalictrum delavayi* 'Splendide White' are among the plants he is going to try there, but he doesn't want to be too hardline about what goes in. 'We have ended up with white in the centre beds but being less hysterical about it round the outside.'

Stavordale is Le Poer Trench's first garden, but over the years there he has learnt to speak its language as fluently as he does Italian and French. Until he was ten, he and his family lived in Hampshire, where he remembers the smell of the greenhouse and growing broad beans on blotting paper in a jam jar. The family

Michael Le Poer Trench, taking a few minutes break from gardening.

emigrated to Australia, and he read Agricultural Science at the University of Queensland, not because he was actually interested in plants, but because it was first in the alphabetical list of science degrees available. 'From that degree I gained a fundamental idea about different types of genetics and the biology of plants but I learned nothing about herbaceous perennials.'

Perhaps it is something to do with his scientific background that he likes to approach things logically, rather than the chuck-it-in-and-let's-see-what-happens attitude of some gardeners. To that end, he does his homework thoroughly, and is constantly talking to plantsmen and designers. After a day outside, he will turn his attention to reading gardening magazines and scouring plant catalogues and the internet for new plants and ideas. 'I do my research. I never stop.'

He not only knows what to plant where and how to look after it, his photographic background and twenty-five years of immersion in the theatrical world have rubbed off too. 'The fantastic thing for me with the garden is the combination of the knowledge – all that stuff to do with pruning and propagating, which you have got to know how to do for it to come out the best – and the other side is the art of it. I see things and go: "That works; that doesn't work." I'm quite instinctive about it.'

The fence around the box balls by the terrace is to protect them from the family dogs.

Part of the art of gardening is also knowing when to step away and let the place relax and do its own thing. Having a thirteenth-century priory at the core of the garden helps dictate this rhythm. 'The great thing about the tumbledown walls and the higgeldy-piggeldy nature is that if there are weeds growing in certain areas – it doesn't matter,' says Le Poer Trench; and adds, 'What I have learned in terms of the feel of the garden is the standard things. It's not rocket science: you mow the lawns, you edge the lawns.' Likewise the neatly clipped topiary, which allows the planting nearby to be more relaxed, and, where the wildflower meadow meets either the gravel or the hedgerow, the gardeners mow a strip round the edge. 'So it looks like you are in charge.'

On the whole Mackintosh takes the part of the appreciative audience. 'The garden is really my baby, but it would be terribly disappointing if he had no interest in it. He won't catch the train up to London without having a good wander in it.' He may not quite remember the names of individual plants, but he notices their effect. Also, as he is a 'super-keen cook', the potager is of special interest: 'He adores the veg garden.'

One thing Mackintosh the impresario is sound on is a sense of drama: look, for example, at the grotto, which appears considerably older than it is. In fact, it was Mackintosh's idea to commission it, and it is now an appropriate last resting place for the bones of monastic inhabitants which were disturbed when the formal pond was being remodelled. He is also in charge of what goes into the pots, which provide vignettes of seasonal colour. And Le Poer Trench will often talk things

A parade of alliums lines the sides of the tiered rill.

through with him when considering design changes in the garden. 'He has very good spatial ideas. Between us, we will come up with something.'

Wander through the 'birthday grove' of trees, given by friends to Le Poer Trench for his fiftieth birthday, and you come to a *coup de théâtre* at the far end of the garden that cannot fail to raise a smile: the 80-foot model of the Bastille elephant, which was used in the 2012 film version of *Les Misérables*. It was always Mackintosh's intention to bring it home. 'What I think is genius is where he has put it,' says Le Poer Trench. It is not stuck out in a field saying "Hello, I'm an elephant!" The idea is that you go, "Oh, I wasn't expecting that." It is exactly what he wanted: hidden from the rest of the garden and from the fields it is in context with the trees. It works brilliantly.'

There are further plans. A whole border will be dug up this autumn, each plant labelled and potted up, and the bindweed removed from the soil before they are replaced. Then there is the gravel and cobble courtyard at the back of the house, which has a sunny, west-facing aspect. He is working on the planting to take advantage of the beautiful low evening light in spring and autumn. 'You could do all sorts of stuff with different grasses and lavenders and things you might not be able to use elsewhere.' So, he's planning *Molinia caerulea* 'Transparent', echinaceas, and early red-flowering peonies, which need space around them, to have their moments in the limelight. As they say, the show must go on.

17 August 2017

DAN PEARSON
& HUW MORGAN

Somerset

As one of the world's most sought-after garden and landscape designers, with clients worldwide, Dan Pearson works as far afield as the Millennium Forest in Hokkaido, Japan and a camphor forest and gardens at the new Amanyangun resort outside Shanghai. He's a busy chap.

One of Pearson's friends recently visited Hillside, the twenty-acre former smallholding near Bath where he has lived since 2010 with his partner, Huw Morgan. 'He said, "What are you going to do with this?" He could only see it as being a responsibility and hours and hours of labour,' says Pearson. You can see the friend's point; not only because at first glance it might look as if he has not yet made the sort of mark on the land one might expect of a celebrated designer – but he has quite enough on his plate with projects for other people.

Then there's *Dig Delve*, their online magazine, in which he regularly writes about gardens, plants and landscaping. A fine cook, Morgan's area is the kitchen garden and recipes. So there's plenty to be getting on with, without having to figure out what to do with Hillside. Would it not just be easier to grow some fruit and veg and enjoy the magnificent views across the valley and beyond?

But Pearson can't help himself, even if it has taken him seven years to start planting up the ornamental beds. It hasn't been seven years of inertia though; he has been working out what to do. His sceptical friend is a talented guitarist, who knows the hours of practice that are necessary to get better at his chosen art. So, too, with the garden; it is a laboratory in which Pearson can work and experiment endlessly (he trialled sixteen varieties of sanguisorba until he found the right ones. Even now, he's not sure about 'Henk Gerritsen', though he will definitely keep 'Red Thunder' and 'Cangshan Cranberry'). 'It's not necessarily about the end products, it is about getting there. If I weren't doing what I am doing here, I wouldn't be able to do my work as well as I can. I would simply be relying on what I learned before. I think I owe that to my work: it needs to be evolving.'

He has certainly been practising for most of his life, designing with plants and gardening since he was five, when he used to help his father at home in Hampshire. He later trained horticulturally at the RHS Garden Wisley, then at the Royal Botanic Garden Edinburgh and Kew. Previously he and Morgan lived in Peckham, south London, where the garden was 130 by 30 feet – large for an urban space but very much its own world, rather than part of a wider landscape.

For many years, Pearson also had Home Farm in Northamptonshire as a place to garden and experiment. It was the subject of a BBC2 series and his 2001 book, *The Garden – A Year at Home Farm*. But when its owner, Frances Mossman, sold it he began to feel 'pot-bound' in Peckham. So he started to look for somewhere where he could work long-term on a larger scale. 'I was in control of every square inch in Peckham, more or less. I knew every single corner like the back of my hand. I wanted to feel more a smaller cog in a bigger wheel, where my mark wasn't as definite, rather than the person who dominated a place: the opposite of being in London.' At first he and Morgan were looking in Sussex and Hampshire. 'It was going to be somewhere there were hills and a countryside that didn't feel too tamed, which is difficult in Britain, and we needed to be within striking distance of London.'

Huw Morgan and Dan Pearson.

After five years of looking, they hadn't found anywhere that was quite right. An old Kew friend who lived near Bath rang him one day in February 2010 to say that the bachelor farmer who lived across the valley had died and his place was about to go on the market. They had never really considered the area, as the friend's house, situated on a north-facing slope, was so blitheringly cold. Nevertheless, 'We came down that weekend. We walked down the slope, over the stream and up the hill into sunshine, as this is a south-facing slope, and we looked back,' Pearson recalls, as we drink coffee in his studio, a former shed where the old boy had died on his tractor, Woody the lurcher basking in the sunlight streaming through the plate-glass window. 'The views and everything were completely different from that perspective; it all ticked. On the way back we had decided. It was a complete surprise but once we had found the place there was no question.'

In a town garden one is usually rather keen to shield out the surroundings; but here the wide views – more than 180 degrees – of gently rolling hills, farmland and woodland are something the couple wanted to embrace from the beginning. 'One of the things Dan was keen to do, which we share, was not to take the site as somewhere you put a house in the middle of a garden and everything is gardened around it,' says Morgan. 'The landscape is so open and the views so amazing that to enclose yourself with hedged or walled gardens would be fighting it. It is about allowing the landscape to be the dominant feature.'

There may now be a loggia by the back door with a low-key outdoor kitchen for summer dining, but they were also keen not to smarten the place up too much, its rough edges and character rubbed away in a wash of Cotswoldy gentrification. 'The house hasn't changed very much. We liked the property because it was a

Verbena bonariensis with *Ridolfia segetum* by water troughs which came originally from a leather tannery in Eastern Europe.

slightly rundown bachelor farmer's place that had been held together with baler twine,' says Morgan. The metaphorical baler twine might have gone and the slopes been levelled and terraced in places in order to make moving around easier, but the ghost of the old farmer would recognize the place – the retaining walls and the studio remain raw breeze block, the rusty corrugated-iron buildings are still standing, looking like they have been cobbled together with whatever the farmer could find lying around his yard.

There was never any question but that Pearson would make his mark on the landscape. It is a tribute to his years of experience that he took his time. 'I have always grown plants and I always will, but I didn't want to make a garden that didn't feel like it was part of the environment.' So, starting on the outer perimeters, the first thing they did was to repair the hedges, plant an orchard, a nuttery and a blossom wood: the things that would take time to grow and give the place a sense of permanence. Improving the heavily grazed landscape for wildlife was also important, so they over-seeded the meadow with wildflowers and worked with the local farmers to develop a regime for hay, as well as fencing off areas to allow the grass to grow longer or allowing woodland to regenerate.

While the house was being renovated and the landscaping squared, they moved into a caravan, bought from a friend for £100. Having already established the soft fruit and vegetable patch on the terrace between the house and the barns, they could at least be surrounded by the oasis of the productive garden while all else was mud and mess. Finally, in the spring of 2017 and after three years of trialling plants to grow in the ornamental area, on the site where the farmer used to grow his cabbages, Pearson started the first phase of planting, the second to come in the autumn of the same year. Taking stock had paid dividends: 'That was really valuable time. It's windy here, it's airy, it's new soil. I think if I had rushed in in the first year I would have made some mistakes.'

The idea is to have an inner core of individual 'moments', while the outer beds will have less detail and pick up the hedge at the top of the garden, or meld into the ditch and fields beyond on the lower edge with the likes of angelicas, persicaria and grasses. As we look out from the studio, a gaura planted in this lower edge is causing him grief – although it seems to be thriving in this damper section, it is too bright for where it sits. 'I'm surprised by how much it feels as if it's in the wrong place. I like it in the central section because that feels higher and drier. So much of this is about the feeling of the plants being right for the place. Everything has got to be like it could be part of this hillside; I can't break that rule just because I want something, otherwise it will change the tone of what I am planting.'

As someone who is not a designer, I am always in awe of how a person can visualize a garden as a whole: it is like writing an orchestral piece for plants, and takes a lifetime of knowledge of their particular habits to do it successfully. Pearson agrees that it is taxing stuff. 'I don't ever feel my brain is being used in quite the same way as when I am doing a planting plan: you use every part of it. It's not an easy thing, as you are trying to imagine form and texture, colour, longevity, short-term, medium-term, seasons and moods. All of those things. You have to pace that through a planting, otherwise it is something that doesn't have a narrative.'

Even world-class designers have their doubts. 'I do have moments when I ask myself: "Why do it, when there is a meadow that is so beautiful just beyond?"' Here the artist's urge kicks in: 'It is a composition that feels like it needs to be made. Maybe one day I will get to the point that I think, "I don't want to do that any more; I just want to be part of something."'

That day is far off at present, though. Pearson is mindful of the time he can give the place, even with extra help two days a week, and has kept the intensive areas to within the curtilage of the house. The rest is a lesson in letting go, to a degree – to allow nettles to grow 7 feet high in places during the summer; one going over with the strimmer later in the year, and it will be accessible again.

'I have been really strict with myself, otherwise it becomes unmanageable. It has to be a joy. That is really, really important,' says Pearson. As he gears up for the next phase of planting and yet more travels to his clients, he says: 'It allows me to feel grounded, this place, and the process of making and gardening it. It is where I feel truly happy. That is the bottom line. It is very simple.'

18 August 2017

Dan Pearson was the first writer I worked with when I became gardening editor at The Sunday Times *in 2000. After many years at another publication, he is back writing for* The Sunday Times *on a quarterly basis. The wheel has come full circle.*

CHRISTOPHER GIBBS

Tangier

Even on the cusp of his ninth decade, Christopher Gibbs modestly professes, 'My goodness, I have a lot to learn,' when it comes to plants in his large north-facing hillside garden in Tangier. 'I'm learning along the way about exotics, about which I used to have a horror.'

What looked out of place in the Oxfordshire garden of his youth is just the thing for a region where rain can be absent for months at a time. 'I remember yuccas at my mother and father's house – I would say, "We must get rid of these horrible yuccas." Now I have thousands.' He's not gone entirely native, however. He's given up on fuchsias, which wilt in the summer temperatures, but he can't resist growing sweet peas and hollyhock, wisteria and roses (*Rosa sanguinea*, *R. mutabilis* and *R. banksia* all do well here, as well as *R. laevigata* 'Cooperi', 'Sir Cedric Morris' and old French varieties). 'They are things I have known all my life.'

That these reminders of English gardens past sit alongside the yuccas, pomegranates and palms, amaryllis and aloes – indeed, the fact he has bothered to make a garden at all in a country where outdoor space is usually seen as somewhere for growing food and crops – is indicative of the comfortable confluence of cultures to which Tangier has been long been host. The city, Morocco's – and Africa's – most north-westerly, looks over the Strait of Gibraltar, where the waters of the Atlantic and the Mediterranean meet: Europe is tantalizingly close.

Tangier has been occupied by various powers over its long history, most recently as an international zone administered by nine different powers over the early twentieth century, before being returned to Moroccan sovereignty in 1956. It has also long been a magnet for louche outsiders and bohemians high and low, and Gibbs, a famously stylish antique collector and dealer, who put the 'swing' into Swinging London in the 1960s, and is friend to the likes of the Rolling Stones, John Paul Getty Junior, Lord Rothschild and Bob Geldof, is the hautest of the haute. It therefore seems appropriate that his home is high on the Old Mountain, the smartest district in town and a few doors down from the King.

When Gibbs first visited in 1958, Tangier was a tenth of the size it is now, and the road outside was a dirt track. The city remained somewhat down at heel for many years, until the ascent to the throne of King Mohammed VI in 1999. Since then, there's been something of a Tangerine renaissance, with a spanky new port and marina being built. With this has come a buying bonanza

Christopher Gibbs, cheerful despite the January chill.

from the international design elite, who do up old houses in the medina and kasbah and are rather keener on the chic than the shabby charms of the city past that posed such allure to Gibbs and his generation.

I tip up chez Gibbs with two mutual friends on a January afternoon and he greets me with a courtly kiss on the hand in a drawing room crammed with books, paintings and beautiful objects. Coats on, as the weather is in its low teens centigrade (it hails the next day, and flattens everything), we set off to explore the garden. Gibbs, his shock of blonde hair white now, grabs a walking stick and makes no concession to his present frail condition as we tour the three acres or so he has been cultivating for the past couple of decades.

The property was formerly the home of Marguerite McBey, the wealthy American widow of Scottish artist James McBey. As a friend of Mrs McBey, who died in 1999, Gibbs knew it well before he bought it in 2000. Other than having a few flowers planted to brighten up the place, neither she nor her husband had been particularly interested in gardening, and they rather resented spending any money on it. 'She was an extremely well-off lady with a very nice house in Holland Park, but she was frugal to the point of folly,' says Gibbs. 'She filled in all the wells with old shoes and rubbish, as she didn't want to mend them.'

He concedes: 'They did initially make a good generous terrace in front and a space for a formal bit which I rejigged in a big way with the help of my friend Umberto Pasti [an Italian writer living nearby, described by a grateful Gibbs as a 'garden boffin and wonder']. There is now a fountain and beds, as well as a huge ancient pomegranate that must have been there for a hundred years.'

Further restructuring and reshaping went on when he bought the former chapel to the house next door a couple of years later and incorporated that and its land, again with the help of Pasti, and that of Cosimo Sesti, an architect with an eye for hard landscaping. There are now several levels, informally connected by winding paths, with the garden unfolding as you walk along.

Gibbs sleeps and works in the chapel, eating and entertaining guests in the original house.

Even in January there are flowers in bloom and one catches the odd whiff of jasmine, a rose lingering on the long pergola above the pool, and paperwhite narcissi underplanting the pomegranate orchard, along with remnants of the native wild daffodils, which flower from November. A *Nicotiana mutabilis* bravely flowers on in one of the many large pots on the terrace and, below, a white iris shows its colour in a newly planted bed. Bulbs play an essential part in the garden: with sheets of *Amaryllis belladonna*, dietes, *Scilla peruviana* and camassias making their appearance through the year.

This is not a garden where everything is smartly presented on a plate, to be viewed as a whole and nature harnessed into obedience. There's something of the ancient philosophers about what Gibbs wants from the different moods and moments he has created; several seating places throughout the garden allow one to contemplate the scene presented, with only birdsong and the regular calls to prayer from distant mosques to distract.

As to what he grows: 'I am a bit snooty about improved varieties and generally go Dame Nature's way in life. I do make exceptions of course, but very few,' says Gibbs, who is rather more knowledgeable about plants than his diffident manner would suggest. 'Having been reared by people whose gossip was all about plants rather than people, I am very interested in plants but I am more interested in gardens as adventure and experience, and surprises: a place to walk and think and reflect.' He adds in a later email: 'There are moments when the garden is bright and colourful and moments when I am glad of the palms and succulents. The garden is very beautiful at night too, with lanterns and lit-up sculpture. Just a few well-placed lumps of ancient Rome always enchant, and things like the pergola covered in wisteria transform, and there are waves of scent from citrus and philadelphus. To me, it is more like painting than collecting.'

Sometimes the focus is close up: perhaps on a bed of irises; an avenue of daturas dangling at eye level, or, as one winds along a path through a shiny carpet of acanthus leaves, coming across a collection of thousand-year-old Jewish headstones dotted among them. 'They came from Ceuta, where they had grubbed up a whole cemetery. Someone arrived with them on the back of a lorry, saying. "Can you use these?" I made a place where you can sit and reflect on the enormous contribution that that the Jews have made to this part of the world.' More tongue in cheek are two eighteenth-century busts – 'Cromwell and King Billy' – keeping watch over the garden from a wall by the pool.

The abundant tree canopy of palms, eucalyptus and cork oaks ('We are trying to replace the pesty mimosas with more long-lived species') shields out the sprawl of the city, though Gibbs uses gaps in the plantation to focus on what he considers important beyond. 'Distant prospects are very important – what the Chinese called "borrowed scenery" – I am very keen on that and framing views.' In one direction he can see mountains; on a fine day Gibraltar and Sierra Nevada are visible, 'and always the mighty Herculean straits and

The wisteria-clad pergola in full bloom, a reminder of English gardens past.

what they call the pillars of Hercules' – the Rock of Gibraltar to the north; Djebel Musa on the Moroccan side.

Across the lane is a doorway in the high wall, which leads to a secret world, with no hint of the city beyond, only mountains and forest glimpsed occasionally. First the service area: compost bins and a shed knocked up by the gardeners made from thinnings and palm fronds to store various mulches ('we are quite keen in the mulch department'). A large clump of aloes with an abundance of red flowers catches the eye – 'very handy for decorating the church at Christmas'. Beyond is a jungle-like garden of meandering paths and a cascade of pools created by a twentieth-century Spanish duke who lived in the Villa Josephine next door, which is now a hotel. It was only discovered when Gibbs and his team cleared the undergrowth of fifty years' neglect by the succeeding owners. With the cooling effect of the water, it is the perfect place to come to escape the summer heat.

As in the main garden, there are plenty of places to stop and contemplate the scene. Down at the bottom, where the soil is very dry and little will grow, is a shelter made from palm fronds and a bench. 'I have got a red lantern off a ship: it is going to be the red light area.' We pass plinths, made by Gibbs from broken

Behind the sculptures of Cromwell and King Billy is the second house, a former chapel, and its palm-filled garden.

pieces of china he has collected. 'They help to articulate space in shady places.' As he is a man of impeccable taste, it is all rather fine. 'My sister comes here and she says: "That is Uncle Alban's service he took to Oxford and that is Aunt Ruth's and that was that beautiful Chinese pot you broke."'

They are a quirky touch in a garden that is born of a love of plants and a confidence to create a sense of place that doesn't have to be on parade all year round: each season has its charms as you walk through – some quiet; others, such as the summer carpet of cosmos, zinnias, nicotiana and *Verbena bonariensis*, rather louder, but confined to a small border in front of the hammam. 'The recipe is quite basic,' says Gibbs. 'Not too many startlements.'

January 2018

GARDENS
OPEN TO THE PUBLIC

NEIL ARMSTRONG
Tremenheere, Penzance, Cornwall
tremenheere.co.uk
Open daily

ISABEL AND JULIAN BANNERMAN
Hanham Court, South Gloucestershire
(no longer theirs)
hanhamcourtgardens.co.uk
Open occasionally
Trematon Castle, Saltash, Devon, their
new garden, is open regularly through the
summer. Visit trematoncastle.com

CAROL BRUCE
Old Bladbean Stud, near Elham, Kent
oldbladbeanstud.co.uk
Open for the NGS on certain days between
Whitsun and the August bank holiday

LOUISE DOWDING
Yews Farm, Martock
louisedowding.co.uk
Open occasionally for the NGS and for
groups of more than twenty

CHRISTINE FACER
Througham Court, Gloucestershire
christinefacer.com
Open by appointment

LORD CHOLMONDELEY
Houghton Hall, Norfolk
houghtonhall.com
The house and gardens are open during the
summer, Wednesday–Sunday

WILLIAM CHRISTIE
The William Christie Garden
Thiré, Vendée, France
jardindewilliamchristie.fr
The garden is open periodically.
Check before you visit.

BELLA AND DAVID GORDON
Plantagenet Plantes
Argentay, Pays de Loire, France
plantagenetplantes.com
Open occasionally and by appointment

JOHN HARRIS
Dewstow Gardens, Caerwent
Monmouthshire
dewstowgardens.co.uk
Open from April to the end of October

ANDY HULME
Crossbones Garden of Remembrance (no
longer his)
London SE1
bost.org.uk
Open daily noon-3 p.m.

JOHN MAKEPEACE
Farrs, Beaminster, Dorset
johnmakepeacefurniture.com
House and garden open by appointment
to groups

JUDITH PILLSBURY
La Louve, Bonnieux, Provence
(no longer hers)
Lalouve.eu
Open to pre-booked groups of ten or more
and on certain days

GERRY ROBINSON
Oakfield Park, Raphoe, Donegal
oakfieldpark.com
Open regularly

WILLIAM WATERFIELD
Le Clos du Peyronnet, Menton
+33 (0) 4 93 35 72 15
Open occasionally by appointment

JANET WHEATCROFT
Craigieburn, Moffat, Dumfries & Galloway
craigieburngardens.co.uk
Open from Easter until the end of October

INDEX

Page numbers in *italics* refer to illustrations

A

Aberglasney, Carmarthenshire
175
Adams, Robert 106, 107–8,
107, 109
Aldeburgh Festival 136
Alsop, Sheila 62, 63, 65
Alsop, Will 62–5, *63*
Amanyangun, Shanghai 194
Ana Tzarev Gallery 97
Ang Diki 27
Architectural Association 80
Argentay, Pays de la Loire,
France 30–5
Armstrong, Neil 9, 88–91, *88*
Arts and Crafts 55, 60, 117
Les Arts Florissants 115
Arundel Castle, West Sussex 58
Ashridge Nurseries 128
Association of Private Pet
Cemeteries and Crematoria
143

B

Bacon, Francis 10
Bailey, Candice 156
Bailey, Rhea 156
Bailey Rae, Corinne 9, 154–7,
155, *157*
Bannerman, Isabel 9, 50,
58–61, *59*
Bannerman, Julian 9, 50,
58–61, *59*
Barenboim, Daniel 136, 140
Baroda, Maharaja of 18
Le Bâtiment, Thiré, France
115–18
Bayley, John 10
Beale, Peter 12
Bell, Clive 22
Bettiscombe, Dorset 174, 176,
177, 179, 184
Birtwistle, Adam 138
Birtwistle, Sir Harrison
136–40, *137*
Birtwistle, Sheila 138, 140
Bisley, Gloucestershire 84–7,
141–4
Black, James 70
Blanch, Lesley 22
Blanchett, Cate 110
Blanchfield, Mhari 50
Blanco, Mark 72

Bledlow, Buckinghamshire
106–9
Bloom, Alan 184
Bockhanger Wood, Kent 131
Bolton Field Naturalists'
Society 163
Bonnieux, Provence 100–5
borrowed scenery 200
Bosdari, Frances de 128
Boyd-Rochfort, Sir Cecil 18
Brabourne, Lord John 128,
129, 131
Bridgeman, Charles 51, 52
British Legion 128, 131
Broadlands, Hampshire 131
Brook, Kelly 9, 167–71, *169*
Brown, Janet 156
Brown, Steve 156, 157
Bruce, Carol 9, 124–7, *124*
Bruce, Maitland 124, 126
Buckingham Palace, London 37
Buckinghamshire, Bledlow
106–9
burials, pet 143–4
Bush, George Sr. 14

C

Camberwell, London 92–4
Campbell, Colen 50
Cap Ferrat, France 95–9
Carnarvon, Lord 18
Carrington, Iona, Baroness
107, 108, *108*, 109
Carrington, Peter, Baron
106–9, *107*
Carter, Howard 18
Carter, Jim 119–23, *120*
Catholic Answers 143
Cavogallo, Peloponnese 14–17
Cecil, Henry 18–21, *19*
Cecil, Julie 18
Chandler, Christopher 98
Chandler, Robert 98
Chandler's Ford, Hampshire
163–6
Chaplin, Charlie 96, 98
Charles, Prince of Wales 50, 58,
87, 128
Charles I, King 68
Charpentier, Marc-Antoine 115
Château Lafite, Médoc, France
184
Chatsworth House, Derbyshire
180

Chatto, Beth 39
Chaumont-sur-Loire, France 34
Chelsea Flower Show 7, 112
medal winning gardeners 9,
58, 114, 132, 145, 148
Chips, Manchester 62
Cholmondeley, Lord David 9,
49–53, *51*, 59
Cholmondeley, George, 5th
Marquess of 51
Cholmondeley, Hugh, 6th
Marquess of 49
Cholmondeley, Lavinia 49
Christie, William 115–18, *118*
Christie's 93, 94, 106
Churchill, Clementine 14
Churchill, Winston 14, 22, 98,
106
Clapham Junction, London
150–3
Clarendon Park, Wiltshire 158
Le Clos du Peyronnet, Menton
22–5, 104, 105
Cocteau, Jean 14
Coleman, Janette 12
Collcutt, Thomas 190
Collector Earl's Garden, West
Sussex 58
Constable, John 75
Cooper, Emily 141
Cooper, Jilly 84–7, *85*, *86*,
141–4, *142*
Cooper, Leo 84, 87, 141
Cooper, Michael 109
Cornwall, Tremenheere 88–91
Cory Manor, Devon 180–4
Country Life Genius of the
Place award 46
Coward, Noël 14, 22
Cox, Stephen 52
Craigieburn, Dumfries &
Galloway 26–9
Crathes Castle,
Kincardineshire 18, 21
Cromwell, Oliver 68
Crosland, Neisha 150–3, *151*
Crosland, Stéphane 151, 153
Crossbones Garden of
Remembrance, London 72–5
Crow, John 75

D

Dacres, Sidney 72, 75
Dahl, Liccy 152

Dahl, Roald 150, 152
Dalai Lama *26*, 27
David Austin Roses 107
  'The Generous Gardener'
    9, 152
Dawa (Daten Ji) *26*, 26–8
Day, Paul 87
Demeter 16, *17*
Devon, Cory Manor 180–4
Dewstow House,
  Monmouthshire 36–8
Deyn, Agyness 110
Diana, Princess of Wales 64,
  110, 112
Dickleburgh, Norfolk 76–9
Dig Delve 194
DiLaura, Simone 97
Dillon, Helen 161
Dodd, Rachael 147
Domesday Book *66*, 68
Donegal, Oakfield Park 44–8
Dorset
  Bettiscombe 174, 176, 177,
    179, 184
  Farrs 80–3
Dowding, Fergus 185, 186
Dowding, Louise 185–9, *186*
Downton Abbey 119, 121, 122,
  123
Dumfries & Galloway,
  Scotland 26–9

E
Edinburgh, Duke of 106, 128
Edward VII, King 50
Egyptians, ancient 143
Elizabeth, Queen Mother 175
Elizabeth II, Queen 143

F
Facer, Christine 54–7, *57*
Farrand, Beatrix 117
Farrs, Dorset 80–3
Fermor, Patrick Leigh 15
Fibonacci sequence 56
Fired Earth 150
Fisher, Charlotte 92, 93, *93*
Fisher, Will 92–4, *93*
FitzGerald, Catherine 158–62,
  159
La Fleur du Cap, Cap Ferrat,
  France 95–9
Flowerdew, Bob 9, 76–9, *77*
Flowerdew, Vonnetta 76, 79
Ford, Henry 40

G
Gallaccio, Anya 52
Garden of Cosmic Speculation,
  Portrack, Dumfries and
  Galloway 55

Gardeners' Question Time
  76, 163
Gardeners' World 163, 167
Garrett, Fergus 9, 145–9, *146*
Geldof, Bob 198
George IV, King 50
Getty, John Paul 14
Getty, John Paul Junior 198
Gibbs, Christopher 198–202,
  199
Gibbs, James 50
Giubbilei, Luciano 9, 145–9,
  145, *146*
Glass, Philip 118
Glenarm Castle, County
  Antrim 158
Glin Castle, County Limerick
  158, 161
Gloucestershire
  Bisley 84–7, 141–4
  Hanham Court 58–61
  Througham Court 54–7
Glover, Brian 158
Golden Section 56
Gordon, Bella 30–5, *31*
Gordon, David 30–5, *31*
Great Dixter, East Sussex
  61, 111, 114, 161, 168
  Luciano Giubbilei & Fergus
    Garrett *frontispiece*,
    9, 145–9
Great Gardens of Cornwall,
  Tremenheere 88–91
Great Storm (1987) *130*, 131
Greenfingers 122
Greenway, Alex 151
Grimshaw, Stewart 180

H
Hadrian 16
Hadspen House, Somerset
  174, 176
Haig, Earl 22
Hammond, Pete 132
Hampshire, Chandler's Ford
  163–6
Hampstead Cricket Club 121
Hampton Court Flower Show
  112
Hanbury, Rose 52
Handley Nursery 21
Hanham Court,
  Gloucestershire 58–61
Hargreaves, Peter 9, 39–43, *40*
Hargreaves, Rose 39, 40, 42
Hargreaves Lansdown 9, 39, 42
Harris, John 36–8, *37*
Harris, Lisa 36
Harris, William 36, 37
Hartropp, Anna 132
Harvey, Gordon 18

Heaffey, Jenny 132
Hein, Jeppe 51
Henson, David 136
Hermès 100
Heywood, Tony 82
Hidcote, Gloucestershire 23, 30
Highgrove, Gloucestershire 50,
  58, 87
Hillier, Sir Harold 165
Hillsborough Castle, Belfast
  162
Hillside, Somerset 194–7
Hinton Manor, Oxfordshire
  66–71
Historic Houses Association
  and Christie's Garden of the
  Year 49
Historic Royal Palaces 162
Hobhouse, Niall 175, 176, 179
Hobhouse, Paul 174
Hobhouse, Penelope 6, *8*, 174–9,
  175, 184, 185
Hockney, David 10
Hoffman, Anthony 55
Holyroodhouse, Palace of,
  Edinburgh 162
Home Farm, Northamptonshire
  194–5
Horner, James 147, 148
Houghton Hall, Norfolk 9,
  49–53, 59
Howard of Rising, Lord 93
Hulme, Andy 72–5, *73*

I
Institute of Horticulture,
  Young Horticulturist of the
  Year 190

J
Jamb 92–3
James Pulham & Sons 36, 37
Jardin Remarquable 100
Jekyll, Gertrude 94
Jencks, Charles 55, 57
Jewson, Norman 55
Jobs, Steve 175
Johnson, Lorraine 138
Johnston, Lawrence 23
Jones, Inigo 58
Jones, Paul 67
Juno 93

K
Keen, Mary 161
Kent
  Kelly Brook 167–71
  Mersham Hatch 128–31
  Old Bladbean Stud 124–7
Kent, William 50, 52
Kew Gardens 67, 70, 194

Kilburn, London 110–14
Kinmonth, Patrick 180–4, *181*
Knatchbull, Michael John 131
Knatchbull, Nicholas 129
Knatchbull, Norton 128, 131
Knatchbull, Patricia 128–31, *129*
Knatchbull, Timothy 129
Koroni castle, Peloponnese 15

L
Lady Gaga 110
Lambert, Alistair 109
Lancaster, Roy 163–6, *166*
Lancaster, Sue 163, 164, 165
Langton, David 190
Langton, Georgia 190
Lansdown, Stephen 39
Last, Andy 132
Lawrence, D.H., *Lady Chatterley* 84
Le Poer Trench, Michael 190–3, *191*
Leeds, Corinne Bailey Rae 154–7
LeGrice, Bill 87
Lennox-Boyd, Arabella 158
Levens Hall, Cumbria 186
Liberace 92
Lindsay, Nancy 23
Linley, Viscount 80
Lloyd, Christopher 61, 120, 147
Lloyd-Webber, Lord 59
London
    Camberwell 92–4
    Clapham Junction 150–3
    Crossbones Garden of Remembrance 72–5
    Jim Carter & Imelda Staunton 119–23
    Kilburn 110–14
    Shepherd's Bush 158–62
Long, Richard 51–2
Lost Gardens of Heligan, Cornwall 38
La Louve, Bonnieux, Provence, France 25, 100–5
Lully, Jean-Baptiste 115
Luther, Martin 144
Lutyens, Edwin 147
Lutyens, Mark 158, 162
Lyde, Bledlow 109

M
McBey, James 199
McBey, Marguerite 199
McCall, Davina 112, 114
McClean, Sir Francis 107
McEwen, Rory 67
McKeown, Jane 20, 21
Mackie, Hamish 87

Mackintosh, Sir Cameron 190, 192, 193
McKnight, Sam 110–14, *111*
Madonna 110
Major, Sir John 132
Makepeace, Jenny 80–3, *81, 82*
Makepeace, John 80–3, *81*
Maktoum, Sheikh Mohammed bin Rashid Al 21
Malins, John 174–5
Mansfield, Katherine 22
Marks & Spencers 132, 133
Marten, Henry 68
Martin, Simon 50
Martock, Somerset *172*, 185–9
Mas St Jérôme, Provence 10–13
Massarella, Louis and Mark 21
Maugham, William Somerset 14, 96
Maxwell, Paul 129
Mee, Margaret 67
memorials, pet 144
Menton, France 22–5, 104, 105
Mere, Wiltshire 136–40
Mersham Hatch, Kent 128–31
Millennium Forest, Hokkaido, Japan 194
Mills, John 69
Minogue, Kylie 110
modernism 15
Mohammed VI, King 198
Monet, Claude 151
Monmouthshire, Wales 36–8
Monument Historique 115
Morgan, Huw 194–7, *195*
Morocco, Tangier 198–202
Moss, Kate 110
Mossman, Frances 194–5
Mountbatten, Lord Louis 128, 129
Mountbatten, Lady Patricia 128–31, *129*
Murdoch, Iris 10
Museum of London 75

N
Naish, Stanley 37
Nash, David 90
    Black Mound 91
National Gardens Scheme (NGS) 7, 9
    Bledlow 109
    Hanham Court 59
    Old Bladbean Stud 126
National Portrait Gallery, *A Gardener's Labyrinth* (2003) 180
National Trust 46, 174–5
National Trust for Scotland 18
Neptune 58
Newmarket, Warren Place 18–21

Newmarket Racecourse, Suffolk 21
Nicolson, Harold 12
Niven, David 96, 98
Niven, Hjordis 98
Norfolk
    Dickleburgh 76–9
    Houghton Hall 9, 49–53, 59
    Sheringham 62–5
Norfolk, Duchess of 58

O
Oakfield Park, Donegal 44–8
Oakley, Henry 37
Obama, President 156
Ocado 133
Old Bladbean Stud, Kent 124–7
Osborne & Little 150
Oudolf, Piet 154, 186
Oxfordshire, Hinton Manor 66–71

P
Parisi, Jeremy 167
Parker, Sarah Jessica 110
Parnham House, Beaminster 80
Pasti, Umberto 199
Patterson, Billy 46
Pays de la Loire, France 30–5, 115–18
Pearson, Dan 9, 194–7, *195*
Peckham Library, London 62, 65
Peloponnese, Greece 14–17
Peto, Harold 151
pets 141, 143
    pet burials 143–4
Petworth House, West Sussex 180
PFMA 143
Pillsbury, Judith 9, 25, 100–5, *101*
Pitcombe, Somerset 176–9
Plant Specialist 151
Plantagenet Plantes 30, 33, 208
Plato 14
Portrack, Garden of Cosmic Speculation, Dumfries and Galloway 55
Provence, France 10–13, 100–5
Pulham, James & Sons 36, 37

R
Rae, Jason 154, 156
Rameau, Jean-Philippe 115
Randall-Page, Peter 109
Raven, Sarah 119
Rees, Martin 56–7
Reiss, Phyllis 175
RHS Garden Wisley, Surrey 37, 158, 175, 194

Ritchie, Lionel 154
Robinson, Gerry 44–8, *44*
Robinson, Heather 44–8
Rose, Stuart 132–5, *133*
Rosebuddies 87
Rossdohan, County Limerick 158
Rothschild, Aline de 49
Rothschild, Lord 59, 198
Rousham, Oxfordshire 143
Royal Academy 62, 64
Royal Botanic Garden Edinburgh 194
Royal Botanic Gardens, Kew 67, 70, 194
Royal College of Art 109
Royal Horticultural Society 11
Victoria Medal of Honour 163, 174
Rug Company 150

S
Saatchi Gallery, London 97, 99
Sackville-West, Vita 10
Sadleir, Michael 55
St Michael's Mount, Cornwall 89
Sander, Jil 175
Sandringham Estate, Norfolk 37, 63, 143
Sassoon, Sir Edward 49
Sassoon, Sybil 9, 49–50, 51, *51, 52*
School of Art, Norwich 79
Scotland, Craigieburn, Dumfries & Galloway 26–9
Seavers, Terry 40
Sellars, Pandora 67
Sesti, Cosimo 199
Shanghai Botanical Garden 163
Shepherd's Bush, London 158–62
Sheringham, Norfolk 62–5
Sherwood, James 67–8, 69, 70
Sherwood, Dr Shirley 66–71, *66*
Shirley Sherwood Gallery of Botanical Art, Kew Gardens 67, 70, 71
Shoup, Charles 14–17, *15*
Shutter, Tim 57
Sinclair, Peter 49
Sir Harold Hillier Gardens, Hampshire 165
Sissinghurst, Kent 12, 30, 50, 104, 111, 124
Smith, Sir Paul 110, 146
Smithers, Peter *164*
Socrates 14
Somerset 39–43
Hadspen House 174, 176

Hillside 194–7
Pitcombe 176–9
Stavordale Priory 190–3
Yews Farm *172*, 185–9
Spender, Lady Natasha 10–13, *10*
Spender, Sir Stephen 10, 11
Stamp, Jez 190
Staunton, Imelda 119–23, *120*
Stavordale Priory, Somerset 190–3
Stirling prize 62
Stratfield Saye, Hampshire 143
Suffolk, Woodbridge 132–5
Suga, Kishio 90
Sussex, Great Dixter 9, 61, 111, 114, 145–9, 161, 168
Sutherland, Graham 22
Sutherland, Guilland 10–11
Sutherland, John 10–11
Swinton, Tilda 110
Sydmonton, Hampshire 59

T
Tangier 198–202
Thatcher, Margaret 106
The Sunday Times 7, 85, 197
The Sunday Times Rich List 49
The Times 141, 143
Thiré, France 115–18
Thompson, Jo *113*, 114
Thompson, Mark 109
Througham Court, Gloucestershire 54–7
Time of Music, Viitasaari, Finland 136
Tintinhull House, Somerset 174–5
Titchmarsh, Alan 39
Tito, Marshal 98
Tollemache, Lord 133
Tollemache, Xa 132, 133, *133*, 134–5
Traeger, Tessa 180–4, *181*
Transport for London 72
Trematon Castle, Cornwall 61
Tremenheere, Cornwall 9, 88–91
Turnell & Gigon 150
Turrell, James 52
Tremenheere 88, 89, 90, 91
Tzarev, Ana 95–9, *96*
Lovers 99

U
Underwood, Paul 50

V
Vanstone, Paul 109
Veitch Memorial Medal 163

Veneto gardens 151
Vésian, Nicole de 100, *102*, 103
Victoria, Queen 63, 128
Victoria Medal of Honour (Royal Horticultural Society) 163, 174
Viking Irish Garden 46
Virago 150
Virgin Mary 75
Vogue 110, 180

W
Waddesdon Manor, Buckinghamshire 37, 50, 59
Wales, Dewstow House, Monmouthshire 36–8
Walmer Castle, Kent 175
Walpole, Horace 52
Walpole, Robert 50, 52
Walter, Sean 151
Warren Place, Newmarket, Suffolk 18–21
Waterfield, Giles 22
Waterfield, Humphrey 22–3, *25*
Waterfield, William 22–5, *23*, 104, 105
Wellington, Duke of 143
Werbowy, Daria 110
West, Dominic 158–62, *159*
Westonbirt Arboretum International Festival of Gardens 55
Westwood, Vivienne 72
Wheatcroft, Andrew 26, 28
Wheatcroft, Janet 26–9, *26*
Wilby, James 49
The William Christie Garden, Thiré, France 115–18
Wiltshire, Mere 136–40
Wisley Gardens, Surrey 158, 175, 194
Wonder, Stevie 154
Woodbridge, Suffolk 132–5
Woolf, Leonard 10
Wright, Elizabeth 46
Wright, Tony 46
Wynter, Billy 91

Y
Yapp, Robin 140
Yews Farm, Martock, Somerset *172*, 185–9

Z
Zatonski, Judy 141

ACKNOWLEDGMENTS

AUTHOR'S ACKNOWLEDGMENTS

My first thanks are to *The Sunday Times* for allowing me to reproduce the articles I have written for the paper, and to all there who have edited and subedited the pieces into shape. A special mention goes to Lucas Hollweg, who preferred food to flowers, and to Carey Scott, Peter Conradi, Karen Robinson and Helen Davies, who have led the Home section over the years.

And thank you too to all the photographers who have made magic out of dull and rainy days to illustrate the interviews and then, often years on, graciously taken the time to rummage through their archives to send me their pictures. I am hugely grateful to them. As I am to the designers and picture editors who have put up with the many demands gardening pages bring.

Jo Christian and Becky Clarke have been a dream to work with at Pimpernel, and my thanks to them, Emma O'Bryen and Gail Lynch for making the whole process so painless.

Lastly, I must thank my mother, Theresa, and all the Theresas in the family before us who have loved gardens and gardening, and have passed down the green gene. This book is for them.

PICTURE CREDITS

The publishers have made every effort to contact holders of copyright works. Any copyright holders we have been unable to reach are invited to contact the publishers so that full acknowledgment may be given in subsequent editions. For permission to reproduce the images on the pages listed below we would like to thank the following.

© Chris Bourchier 19, 20–21
© Mark Bourdillon 77
© Vicki Couchman 93, 120, 122–3, 133, 134
© Rachel Denning 68, 70–71
© Bob Flowerdew, 78
© Francesco Guidicini 159
© Harpur Garden Library 51, 53, 63, 64
© Peter Hinwood, 201, 202
© Sayaka Hirakawa 73
© John Lawrence 107, 108
© Michael Le Poer Trench 193
© Andrew Montgomery/Luciano Giubbilei frontispiece, 146, 149
© Huw Morgan 196
© Elizabeth Novick 181
© Gerry Robinson 44, 45, 47
© Adrian Sherratt 54, 56, 57, 59, 60, 81, 82, 83, 85, 86, 137, 139, 142
© Peter Tarry 129, 130
© Tessa Traeger 182–3
© Simon Upton/Jamb 94, 95
© Sven Vandenbosch, 96, 99

JACKET PHOTOGRAPHS
FRONT: Border at Great Dixter by Luciano Giubbilei (©Andrew Montgomery/Luciano Giubbilei)
BACK, TOP ROW, L–R: Fergus Garrett & Luciano Giubbilei (©Andrew Montgomery/Luciano Giubbilei); Catherine FitzGerald & Dominic West (© Francesco Guidicini); Kelly Brook
SECOND ROW, L–R: Julian & Isabel Bannerman (© Adrian Sherratt); Huw Morgan & Dan Pearson; Corinne Bailey Rae
THIRD ROW, L–R: Jim Carter & Imelda Staunton (© Vicki Couchman); Bob Flowerdew (© Mark Bourdillon); Andy Hulme (© Sayaka Hirakawa); William Christie.
BOTTOM ROW, L–R: Jilly Cooper (© Adrian Sherratt); alliums in Michael Le Poer Trench's garden (© Michael Le Poer Trench)

All other photographs © Caroline Donald